Ready

FINDING THE COURAGE TO FACE THE UNKNOWN

A Six-Week Study on Joshua 1-5

HEATHER MARSHALL DIXON
THE RESCUED LETTERS

READY: FINDING THE COURAGE TO FACE THE UNKNOWN

Published by Heather Dixon, © 2017 Heather Dixon

Printed in the United States of America
First Printing, 2017

ISBN-13: 978-1546519010 ● ISBN-10: 1546519017

To order additional copies of this resource, order online at www.amazon.com or visit www.therescuedletters.com for more information.

Cover design by Heather Dixon, artwork provided by Graphic Safari.

The Rescued Letters
www.therescuedletters.com

Dedication

To Grandma Letha, my true Elishama:
Thank you for showing me what real faith looks like. And for
giving me my first Bible. I've never let go of it.

Contents

About the Author
About the Study
Introduction

About the Author

Diagnosed with an incurable and terminal genetic disorder that she inherited from her mother, Heather is no stranger to the spiritual battlefield. Choosing to hope in God's plan for her life, she writes at The Rescued Letters, offering encouragement and equipping women to trust in God, face their greatest fears, and choose life, especially when life presents its most difficult circumstances. When she's not spilling rescued letters all over the place, you might find her cooking for her husband and son, brainstorming all the possible ways to organize legos and superheroes, checking out way too many library books, writing for a few other blogs, or unashamedly indulging in her love for all things Disney.

Heather is a regular contributor to LifeWay's Journey Magazine and a Proverbs 31 Ministry-She Speaks graduate.

www.therescuedletters.com
equipping women for courageous living

About the Study

THE READY STUDY is a six-week study, designed to equip you for courageous living. To do that, this study has several levels of participation intended to meet you right where you are in your faith journey.

Here's what you'll find within each week:

- An **optional video teaching session** to prime your heart and mind for what you will study on your own throughout each week. You'll find a blank section at the beginning of each week to help you jot down any notes from the session.
- An **excerpt from the Joshua Diary** - The Joshua Diary is a creative narrative, based on a biographical sketch of Joshua that I composed while writing this study. It's grounded in Biblical facts and written from Joshua's perspective, but remember that it is only a fictional retelling of pieces of Joshua's life. It is meant to give you a small glimpse into the heart of a man that lived and breathed and put himself on the front line for God over and over again. I recommend that you read the Joshua Diary excerpts as devotional content before you begin your assignments for that particular week.
- Five days of **weekly homework assignments** - If we want to hear from God, we've got to be in His Word. There isn't an easy way around this. To get the most out of this study, this is where you'll want to spend the bulk of your time. You won't remember that nifty quote from the teaching session, but you will remember that ah-ha moment you had with God in the quiet of your heart as you delved deeper into His Word. Each day's assignment begins with a devotional prompt, which is followed by questions to lead you through your personal study of God's Word. Answer the questions as you can and remember to cover yourself in grace. God does this already for you every day. Grace is a good thing.

At the back of this study, you'll find:

- Tips and resources for studying the Bible on your own.

I recognize that certain stages of life allow for certain levels of participation with this sort of thing. Over the past twenty-five years, I have caffeinated my way through 18-hour course loads at college, 60-hour work weeks in my full-time job while also mothering my full-time toddler, and 24-hour you're-a-stay-at-home-mom-now-so-you-don't-get-a-break days. Finding just five spare minutes for Bible study presented a challenge during those days. I've also seen times during quieter seasons of life that allowed for 3+ hours every day in God's Word. I understand different times call for different commitments.

This study is designed to meet you where you are. With God's guidance, only you can determine the level of participation that suits your season of life. Remember to strive for the maximum amount of time in God's Word with the least amount of anxiety. What works for your fellow Bible study sisters may not work for you. Whatever you decide, I hope you'll find that the more you study His Word, the less anxious you will feel.

Here are the levels of participation for this study:

> LEVEL 1: Read Joshua 1-5 and participate in the teaching sessions only.

> LEVEL 2: Read Joshua 1-5 and participate in the teaching sessions.
> Read the Joshua Diary.

> LEVEL 3: Read Joshua 1-5 and participate in the teaching sessions.
> Read the Joshua Diary.
> Read the devotional content at the beginning of each daily assignment.

> LEVEL 4: Read Joshua 1-5 and participate in the teaching sessions.
> Read the Joshua Diary.
> Read the devotional content at the beginning of each daily assignment.
> Answer the questions for each daily assignment.

After prayerfully considering your season of life and how God is leading you in this study, which level of participation seems to be the best fit for you?

1   2   3   4

One final word: courageous living doesn't happen overnight and it doesn't happen without the study of God's Word and the help of the Holy Spirit. Be in the Word. Be faithful in prayer. And be bold in asking for the Spirit to move in you. I guarantee you that He will.

Ready?

> Use the hashtag #READYSTUDY on social media to connect with other women walking through this study.

Introduction

A LETTER TO MY FELLOW WARRIORS

If you had told me a year and a half ago that I would be writing a Bible study on Joshua, I would have laughed out loud. Loudly.

Well, I might not have actually laughed just yet because a year and a half ago I was on a ventilator as my surgeon was delicately plugging coils of platinum into my head in an effort to repair my ruptured carotid artery. Essentially, she was creating a clot, a man-made dam to stop the flow of blood which no longer had any boundaries.

In the first five chapters of Joshua, we'll see God create the same thing for the Israelites at the bank of the flooding Jordan. Except this dam isn't man-made and it isn't made of platinum. It's made of solid, supernatural, divine power by a God who longs to do the same thing for you.

This study was born out of God's gracious warning to me just before my carotid artery ruptured and I was later diagnosed with Vascular Ehlers-Danlos Syndrome, an incurable and terminal genetic connective tissue disorder. His warning was simply this: *Get Ready.*

Wanting to confirm what I had heard with His Word, I found myself in the first few chapters of Joshua. But as I studied more, I discovered God's message to get ready coming alive throughout the entire Bible. It's a message that is relevant to our here and now, and also to our future. It's God's plan for the woman who knows the battle is coming, but refuses to leave the front line. But here's the good news: the blessing lies just beyond the battle. Lean in and hang on, sisters. God is ready to meet you in these pages.

Know that with every word here, I am waging war for you. More importantly, so is your heavenly Father.

Much Love,

Heather

A Prayer for the Ready Warrior

Psalm 91 has often been hailed as the "soldier's prayer." Stories abound of modern-day soldiers being kept safe in the fiercest of battles as they recited this Psalm daily or kept a print of it tucked somewhere in their armor. You can probably see why I chose to include Psalm 91 at the beginning of our study on Joshua. It's promises of divine protection are powerful.

But there is another reason why Psalm 91 is at the start of our journey.

If you are new to Bible study (or maybe even if you're not), you may not be aware that the canonized Bible (the Bible that you are holding near you right now) is not organized chronologically. It starts with Genesis and ends with Revelation and you can always find the Psalms smack dab in the middle. But all of the Psalms weren't written smack dab in the middle of Biblical times; when organized chronologically, you will find them throughout much of the Old Testament, and not always in numerical order.

We don't definitively know the author of Psalm 91. But we do know that the author of Psalm 90 is Moses. When Moses died, he passed the reins on to Joshua as leader of the Israelites. We'll look at this a little more later in the study, but for now, just know that Moses was Joshua's most prominent teacher and mentor. Second only to God, Moses was surely Joshua's hero.

Several Biblical commentators agree that based on historical literacy traditions, it is very likely that because we know that Moses wrote Psalm 90, we can also attribute the authorship of Psalm 91 to him as well.

Go ahead and turn in your Bibles to the first chapter of Joshua. Now turn back one page to the book just before it. You should be in Deuteronomy 34. Chronologically, this is precisely where Psalm 91 should live - right between Deuteronomy and Joshua. Right between Moses' death and Joshua's calling.

Here's where I am going with this, sisters: if Moses did indeed write Psalm 91, then it is very likely that its words are some of the last words that Joshua would hear from his earthly hero. **These are the words spoken from one warrior to another, on the cusp of the biggest battle of his life.**

I am praying these verses over each of you. Let the words of Psalm 91 be what we speak to and over ourselves as we proceed with this study.

Welcome to the battle.

PSALM 91

The one who lives under the protection of the Most High
dwells in the shadow of the Almighty.
I will say to the Lord, "My refuge and my fortress,
my God, in whom I trust."
He Himself will deliver you from the hunter's net,
from the destructive plague.
He will cover you with His feathers;
you will take refuge under His wings.
His faithfulness will be a protective shield.
You will not fear the terror of the night,
the arrow that flies by day,
the plague that stalks in darkness,
or the pestilence that ravages at noon.
Though a thousand fall at your side
and ten thousand at your right hand,
the pestilence will not reach you.
You will only see it with your eyes
and witness the punishment of the wicked.
Because you have made the Lord—my refuge,
the Most High—your dwelling place,
no harm will come to you;
no plague will come near your tent.
For He will give His angels orders concerning you,
to protect you in all your ways.
They will support you with their hands
so that you will not strike your foot against a stone.
You will tread on the lion and the cobra;
you will trample the young lion and the serpent.
Because he is lovingly devoted to Me,
I will deliver him;
I will protect him because he knows My name.
When he calls out to Me, I will answer him;
I will be with him in trouble.
I will rescue him and give him honor.
I will satisfy him with a long life
and show him My salvation.

Week One

JOSHUA 1

AGAIN, IF THE TRUMPET DOES NOT SOUND A CLEAR CALL, WHO WILL GET READY FOR BATTLE?

1 CORINTHIANS 14:8 NIV

Teaching Session One
A NEW WAY

The Joshua Diary

EVEN SO

The ground is still fresh, Lord. This dark mound of dirt still curves above the flat of the earth, the grave below it has not yet settled.

I know what they say. Some of my men say it is the first step onto the field. Some say it is the sound of the clashing swords. Some say it is the forced retreat when loss is imminent. But I know that the hardest part of any battle is this fresh ground. It taunts at our lives and breaths and souls as if to say *I am waiting for you.* I know we are but dust. The graves of your people surround me. Even so, I know you are a maker of ways.

He was my teacher, my mentor, my master. He was my friend. Was the ground as fresh as this when you buried him? And will I ever know an earthly hero as great as he? It was my voice that carried his victory cry over the Amalekites. It was my hand that scribed his prayers. It was my face that he saw after meeting yours on the mountain. I weep for him, still.

He was your man, your servant, your prophet. He was your friend. Will there ever be another man of dust to rise up as he did for you? I cannot imagine it. And so I weep for the spacious place you showed him that he would never know on this earth. He saw, but did not know. How badly did I want him to know this blessing place! Even so, his greatest concern remained for your people, that they might have a shepherd when he was gone.

I held my breath as he firmly laid his gnarled fingers around my shoulders, the fragile and furrowed skin betraying the strength he still possessed. Through his hands I received your blessing. And through his hands I received your call. Eleazar, the priest, watched. And Eleazar inquired of you on my behalf so that I might hear your Word. I long to hear from you. Even so, will I be worthy of this calling? Lord, I want to be worthy.

I am your soldier, your servant, your son. Lord, let me be your friend. The days of weeping and mourning here will come to an end. There is new ground to conquer, I know, but this ground in Moab is still fresh. It haunts me. We need a new way, Lord. I do not want to shovel fresh ground anymore, lest it be for planting and harvesting and setting firm foundations into rich soil that we can call our own.

I do not know the way, Lord. Even so, I will rise from this fresh ground. Because I know that you do.

DEUTERONOMY 34
NUMBERS 27:12-23

Day One
A MAKER OF PROMISES

I cringed as I heard the footsteps come down the stairs that morning. My ten-year-old son would be expecting me to take him to a consignment sale that day. Of all things, he somehow thinks that consignment sales are the pinnacle of shopping experiences. You know, the ones where sleep-deprived mothers cart in every imaginable piece of gently-used clothing and toys in all the laundry baskets they own? It's a sea of ponytails, marching forward in an effort towards good stewardship as they hope to sell some of their children's used items. And all of this so they can turn right back around and reinvest their profits into a wardrobe that will only last six months. Been there. Still there, actually. Anyone in the market for size 10 slims?

Although he has accompanied me to the "drop-off" portion of a consignment sale, I've never taken Thomas to an actual sale where you get to purchase things. I had promised him that I would take him to the consignment sale that weekend, but alas, life happened. We could not go. I would have to break my promise and it broke my heart to do it.

Thankfully, we serve a God who has never had to utter those words. If we are about to learn anything from the story of Joshua it is this: God is a promise-keeper. Faithful to the very end, God is serious about keeping His word. He will not forget. He will not change His mind. Take that with you into your day today. God will never break His promise.

Before we settle ourselves into the story of Joshua, we need to understand the story of God's people. Namely, the Israelites. And to understand the story of the Israelites, we have to go all the way back to 2091 BC, in the first book of the Bible.

Turn in your Bibles to **Genesis 11 and read Genesis 11:31 – 12:9.**

What did God promise Abram?

What did God ask Abram to do?

If there is a heading in your Bible for this section, write it here:

_____

If you look back at **Genesis 11:31** you'll see that Abram was from Ur. Ur of the Chaldeans, to be exact.

Ur was a city in southern Mesopotamia, in what is now modern-day, southeastern Iraq. Canaan was a region far west of Ur, in what is now known as parts of Israel, Palestine, Lebanon, Syria, and Jordan. To travel from Ur to Canaan, Abram and his family would follow the Euphrates River to the northwest and then after a brief stopover in Haran, they would travel southwest into Canaan.

The journey would take Abram through approximately 950 miles of the unknown, all set in motion by a calling from His heavenly father.

Take a look back at **Genesis 12:1-5**. Who travelled with Abram on his journey to Canaan? _____

_____

And who *didn't* travel with Abram? _____

_____

_____

Sometimes God calls us into uncharted territory. And sometimes, as in the case of Abram, God calls us into that uncharted territory almost nearly *alone*.

Can you think of a time when God called you completely out of your comfort zone?

_____

_____

_____

_____

_____

We're about to see that when God calls us out of our comfort zone, He always has a plan...and a promise.

Read **Genesis 13:14-17** below:

> After Lot had separated from him, the Lord said to Abram, "Look from the place where you are. Look north and south, east and west, for I will give you and your offspring forever all the land that you see. I will make your offspring like the dust of the earth, so that if anyone could count the dust of the earth, then your offspring could be counted. **Get up** and walk around the land, through its length and width, for I will give it to you."

GENESIS 13:14-17

The land that the Lord mentions here in **Genesis 13** is Canaan. The Promised Land. This is the uncharted territory that God called Abram to. Think back on your answers from the first two questions for today: *What was God's promise to Abram and what did God ask Abram to do?*

Why do you think it was necessary for Abram to travel into uncharted territory in order for God to bless him greatly?

Now, circle the bolded words in the last sentence above from **Genesis 13:14-17**. We'll come back to these words later in the study, but for now, we must careen forward through the pages of history to land ourselves in 1406 BC, at the start of our Joshua story. Joshua is about to conquer the Promised Land.

Wait a minute. Didn't God already settle His people in the Promised Land?

Look back at **Genesis 11:31 – 12:9**. God asked Abram to travel from Ur to _____. What happened in the 685 years between 2091 BC and 1406 BC that took God's people out of the Promised Land?

To answer that question, let me introduce you to a few key characters:

Meet Joseph, Abraham's (that would be God's new name for Abram) great-grandson. Read **Genesis 37:36** below and circle the place where Joseph had been sold.

Meanwhile, the Midianites sold Joseph in Egypt to Potiphar, an officer of Pharaoh and the captain of the guard.

GENESIS 37:36

So now after three generations of living in the Promised Land, the Israelites are in *Egypt*, not Canaan. And as it turns out, Egypt is not a happy place for the Israelites. But remember, God has a plan and a promise...

Meet Moses, Joseph's nephew. Moses is about to meet God in a burning bush. Read **Exodus 3:7-10** below and underline what God says about the Promised Land.

Then the LORD said, "I have observed the misery of My people in Egypt, and have heard them crying out because of their oppressors, and I know about their sufferings. I have come down to rescue them from the power of the Egyptians and to bring them from that land to a good and spacious land, a land flowing with milk and honey--the territory of the Canaanites, Hittites, Amorites, Perizzites, Hivites, and Jebusites. The Israelites' cry for help has come to Me, and I have also seen the way the Egyptians are oppressing them. Therefore, go. I am sending you to Pharaoh so that you may lead My people, the Israelites, out of Egypt."

EXODUS 3:7-10

Moses does indeed lead the Israelites out of Egypt, but he doesn't lead them home. The Israelites would wander for 40 years in the desert before they get close to entering the Promised Land again. But remember, with every promise, God always has a plan. And we are about to see God make a new way in order to keep His promise.

WHEN GOD MAKES A PROMISE, HE ALWAYS HAS A PLAN.

If you listened to the teaching session from this week, recall your thoughts and notes on the awareness that God is a maker of ways. Is there a prayer that you have been praying recently, asking God to make a way for something? _____

_____

_____

Does knowing that God is a promise-keeper change how you pray this prayer? ___

_____

_____

_____

_____

If so, rewrite your prayer here, and close this day by offering your prayer to God.

Day Two
THE MAN, THE MYTH, THE LEGEND

I spent spring break of my senior year with my grandparents. When your grandmother cooks chicken pastry like mine does, it's just what you do.

My grandparents were the first to show me what true faith looks like. They gave me my first Bible. They took me to church. And before I was mature enough to realize it, they planted a love for God's Word deep in my heart.

I've heard my grandmother pray for our family. She taught me to talk to Jesus just like He was in the room, because He always is. I've watched my grandmother bury her youngest daughter, my mother. After that she regularly served with the Hospice organization, sitting quietly with and prayerfully ushering those near death from this life to the next. I've felt her weathered hands along my shoulder as we cried together for just a moment, and then nodded with her as she briskly told me, "enough tears for now. Time to move on."

I am blessed to have been born into a family full of strong women. *Weak* has never been a word used to describe the female members in my bloodline. But if you ask me who first taught me how to live courageously, I will always answer: my grandma Letha. She will be quick to tell you that her courage doesn't flow from an earthly source. She finds her strength in the Lord.

Joshua, as we are about to see, knew what it was like to watch and learn from his grandparent. He also knew what it was like to fully depend on the Lord for strength and courage.

AFTER THE DEATH OF MOSES THE LORD'S SERVANT, THE LORD SPOKE TO JOSHUA, SON OF NUN, WHO HAD SERVED MOSES.

JOSHUA 1:1

When God spoke to Joshua after Moses' death, Joshua was approximately 80 years old. Let that sink in for a minute. And then imagine the multitude of experiences one might have had in 80 years that would prepare you for your ultimate calling. Because that's just what God did over the course of 80 years: He prepared Joshua for his true calling.

We will see together tomorrow how Joshua's work with Moses prepared him for his calling. But there was someone else in Joshua's life that helped to mold him from the day he was born.

Let's get ready to meet him:

Joshua the (Grand) Son

Read **Joshua 1:1**. Who is Joshua's father? _____

The Bible doesn't give us a lot of information about Joshua's father. We know that Nun was from the tribe of Ephraim and that he was likely a fisherman, but that's about it. We know a little bit more about Joshua's grandfather.

Read **1 Chronicles 7:20-27** and note in verse 26: who was Nun's father? _____
_____

Let's take a closer look at what we know about Elishama. Read **Numbers 1:1-16**.

This command from the Lord was given as a part of the final preparations required of the Israelites in order to conquer the Promised Land. What was Elishama being designated to do? _____
_____

Flip a few pages further in your Bibles to **Numbers 2:18**. Now what was Elishama's role? _____
_____

And one more: Read **Numbers 7:48-53**. Describe what Elishama was doing in this passage: _____
_____
_____
_____

In these three passages from Numbers, we see a glimpse of the grandfather Joshua watched his entire life. Elishama, Moses' helper for the census. Elishama, leader of the Ephraim tribe. Elishama, the offering giver. Each of these roles were regarded with much respect among the Israelites. You weren't chosen for these roles unless you were an honorable man who was faithful to the Lord.

Can you imagine what it must have been like for Joshua to watch his grandfather perform these tasks? To know that of the 40,500 war-ready men in the Ephraim tribe, your grandfather was the one chosen to lead them alongside Moses?

We'll see more of this as we get deeper into this study, but Joshua was nothing if he was not a man of faith. We don't know for sure, but I cannot help but conclude that Joshua's faith was shaped by watching his grandfather. Did they have talks at sunrise about the character of God? Did Elishama give him advice on how to lead men with godly character and integrity? Did they encourage one another over dinner with the promises of what was to come in Canaan? We can only imagine, but my guess would be a resounding yes to all of the above.

What about you? Who in your life is your Elishama? Who has played a significant role in shaping you into the woman you are today? It may or may not be someone connected to you by blood. If someone (or more than one) comes to mind, write their names here: _____

_____

In what ways have they helped build your faith or your character? _____

_____
_____
_____
_____
_____

Here's the one thing that floors me about Joshua and Elishama: Long before Joshua was called to lead the Israelites, God provided what Joshua would need to prepare him for that calling. God knew that Joshua would need an upright, godly man to show him how to lead. Certainly, Joshua would see this example lived out in Moses. But he would see it from the moment he drew his first breath in his own flesh and blood.

LONG BEFORE GOD CALLS YOU, HE PREPARES YOU.

Think about the job or role that you are fulfilling right now. Now think about how what you are doing might affect God's kingdom. What are some of the ways that God has prepared you for what you are doing right now? _____

_____
_____
_____
_____
_____
_____
_____
_____

His relationship with his grandfather was not the only way that God prepared Joshua for the biggest calling on his life. This portion is optional, but if you'd like to delve a little further into Joshua's life before God called Him to get ready, take a look at the chart below.

Pick one experience from Joshua's life, read the corresponding scripture passage, and complete the chart with how you think that experience helped Joshua prepare for the unknown to come.

Experience	Scripture Passage	What did Joshua observe or participate in?	What do you think Joshua learned from this experience?
Joshua as a slave	Exodus 7-12 or Exodus 14-15		
Joshua as a soldier	Exodus 17:8-16		
Joshua as a servant	Exodus 24:12-18 and Exodus 32:1-18		
Joshua as a spy	Numbers 13 and Numbers 14:1-10		
Joshua as a successor	Deut 3:21-29 and Deut 31:1-8 and Deut 31:23		

Day Three
MOSES IS DEAD

The customer rang the bell from behind the counter. I hustled to the front from the back of the bakery. The manager had taken off that afternoon and I was the only one in the little sweet shop. Expecting to help the customer choose a cookie or a cupcake for an afternoon treat, I was shocked when she asked for her daughter's birthday cake.

We had no birthday cakes that were decorated and ready to go in the freezer in the back. I checked again, just to be sure. No. No decorated birthday cakes. I apologized profusely to the mother while my brain furiously tried to come up with a suitable solution. The bakery's owner had forgotten to decorate the cake.

I was the cookie baker. This was my role. Arrive early. Cream the butter, sugar, and eggs. Add flour and seasonings. Roll, cut, spoon the cookies onto the baking sheet and into the oven they go. And repeat. Newbie baker that I was, I had not graduated to the cake-decorating role as of yet. But the frazzled mother was standing in the bakery on her way to Sayer's fourth birthday party. I could not let her leave empty-handed.

Twenty minutes later, I emerged from the back, covered in powdered sugar and pink icing. Sayer would have her birthday cake. That was the day I learned that I had a bit of talent in the cake-decorating arena.

Sometimes, we are prepared for the unknown and sometimes we are thrust into it blindly. Either way, we would be wise to recognize when it's our turn to take the lead. If we're listening, God will tell us when it's time.

"MOSES MY SERVANT IS DEAD. NOW THEN, YOU AND ALL THESE PEOPLE, GET READY TO CROSS THE JORDAN RIVER INTO THE LAND I AM ABOUT TO GIVE TO THEM—TO THE ISRAELITES.

JOSHUA 1:2 NIV

Turn in your Bibles to **Joshua 1 and read verses 1-2.**

I am quite certain that Joshua did not need God to inform him that Moses was, in fact, dead. Take a look at **Joshua 1:1.** What was Joshua's job? _____

_____

As Moses' aide since youth, Joshua was the official assistant for the leader of Israel. Joshua was a warrior, by default. But as Moses' aide, he also had to learn the ways of God and the holy laws given to the Israelites. He was the only person allowed to accompany Moses partway up the mountain when Moses received the law at Mount Sinai. (**Exodus 24:12-18**) He was responsible for guarding the special tent where Moses met with God. (**Exodus 33:7-11**) He was jealous for Moses' authority (**Numbers 11:26-30**) and also, as we will see, for the authority of God.

So I find it hard to imagine that Joshua was learning about Moses' death for the first time when the Lord spoke to him in **Joshua 1:2**. Rather, I think God used these three words, *Moses is dead*, as a reminder to Joshua: a reminder that it was his turn to lead.

Can you recall a time when you had to take the lead in place of someone else? ___

_____
_____
_____

How did you feel about the person who had led before you? _____

_____
_____
_____

It is traditionally accepted that the book of Deuteronomy was written by Moses, with the exception of the portion at the end about his death. Most scholars agree that this final portion of Deuteronomy was written by Joshua.

Read **Deuteronomy 34:1-12**.

Paying particular attention to the fact that Joshua wrote this about Moses, use the space below to write specific words that might describe how Joshua felt about Moses.

Joshua had been called by God to be Moses' successor as the leader of the Israelites. This would involve war battles, unwavering leadership, protecting the people of God, and encouraging them forward towards the Promised Land. And he would do all of this with Moses' looming shadow in his mind.

What do you think would be the hardest part of this calling for Joshua? And why?

_____

_____

_____

_____

_____

_____

Can you think of someone in your life that you would describe in the same way that Joshua described Moses? _____

Sisters, if you have a Moses in your life, rejoice that God has given you someone godly to emulate. But know this: God has designed and equipped you to do a very specific job at a very specific time in a very specific place. Your Moses can't do it. But you can.

There was a reason that God allowed the reins to be passed on to Joshua (remember our Day 1 lesson – God had a plan to fulfill His promise). But Joshua couldn't be Moses, and neither can we. With God's guidance, we must chart our own course. You must be solely and exactly who God designed you to be, and not someone else.

GOD HAS DESIGNED AND EQUIPPED YOU TO DO A VERY SPECIFIC JOB AT A VERY SPECIFIC TIME IN A VERY SPECIFIC PLACE.

Turn in your Bible to **Ephesians 2 and read verse 10**. Rewrite this verse in your own words here:

Now choose two of the following verses to read. Rewrite them in your own words in the space provided to the right.

PSALM 119:73-74

ISAIAH 64:8

JEREMIAH 1:4-5

PSALM 139:15-16

1 PETER 4:10-11

Take a few moments to pause and seek the Lord's guidance in prayer. Ask Him to confirm or reveal to you the gifts He has given specifically to you. Take your time here. You may need to sit on this for a while and come back to answer this later.

When you are ready, write anything that the Lord revealed to you below. If more questions arose, rather than answers, that's okay too. Write them down and continue to seek the Lord's will on this.

If you know that God is definitely calling you to take the lead on something, write it here:

It's my turn to _____

Day Four
GET READY TO RISE

I was sitting on our screened-in porch listening to the early morning songs of my backyard bird friends when God told me to *get ready*.

The morning breeze rustles the pages of my Bible, given to me by my grandparents almost twenty-seven years ago on the Christmas just after my mother died, and I close my eyes. I take a deep breath and with every exhale, one by one, I push away the scattered thoughts running through my mind. This takes time.

I begin to see the words of **Psalm 119:105** floating behind closed eyelids and this is where I stay. Inhale. Exhale. Listen.

Get ready, Heather.

Wanting to confirm what I had heard with God's Word, I looked up the first time those two words appeared in my NIV Bible. As it turns out, I wasn't the first person to hear the words *get ready* from God. Joshua heard them also.

As I studied more into God's Word about *getting ready*, I had a solid awareness in my gut that something was coming. Tom and I knew that I was about to miscarry our second child. I was pregnant, but my body had not recognized the loss just yet, so we were just waiting for the miscarriage process to start. But still...I sensed that there was something bigger coming down the road and God needed to prepare me for it.

What I learned is what you are studying now: that (1) God speaks to us directly through His Word, and (2) that God calls us to stay ready for whatever is to come. So if you are wondering how in the world you can wake up tomorrow morning with the courage to face the unknown, read on sisters.

MOSES MY SERVANT IS DEAD. NOW THEN, YOU AND ALL THESE PEOPLE, GET READY TO CROSS THE JORDAN RIVER INTO THE LAND I AM ABOUT TO GIVE TO THEM—TO THE ISRAELITES.

JOSHUA 1:2 NIV

Turn in your Bibles to **Joshua 1 and read verses 1-2**. Yes, I know we did this yesterday. Bear with me.

Circle the bolded words in **Joshua 1:2** below.

Moses my servant is dead. Now then, you and all these people, **get ready** to cross the Jordan River into the land I am about to give to them—to the Israelites.

JOSHUA 1:2 NIV

If I hadn't made this clear as mud by now, these two words are the official launching pad of our study. When I sat on my back porch, researching the first times these words appeared in my Bible, I landed right here in **Joshua 1:2**.

Let's look a little closer at the words *get ready*. When studying God's Word, we can often find a deeper understanding of it when we look at different translations of a particular passage.

Read **Joshua 1:2** in each of the different translations below and circle the word or words used for *get ready*.

NEW INTERNATIONAL VERSION

Moses my servant is dead. Now then, you and all these people, get ready to cross the Jordan River into the land I am about to give to them--to the Israelites.

NEW KING JAMES VERSION

Moses My servant is dead. Now therefore, arise, go over this Jordan, you and all this people, to the land which I am giving to them--the children of Israel.

NEW LIVING TRANSLATION

Moses my servant is dead. Therefore, the time has come for you to lead these people, the Israelites, across the Jordan River into the land I am giving them.

HOLMAN CHRISTIAN STANDARD BIBLE

31

Moses My servant is dead. Now you and all the people prepare to
cross over the Jordan to the land I am giving the Israelites.

What word does your Bible use? _____

Write the words that you circled and the word from your Bible, if different, here:

Looking at these words used in different translations for *get ready*, describe in
your own words what you think God was asking Joshua to do: _____
_____
_____
_____
_____

We can go even deeper into our understanding of God's Word by looking at the
original word used in the Bible. For the most part, the Old Testament was written
in Hebrew and the New Testament was written in Greek. The Hebrew word used
for *get ready* in **Joshua 1:2** is QUM.

QUM is a verb that means *to arise or stand up*.

Why do you think God chose this word when instructing Joshua in verse 2? _____
_____
_____
_____
_____

This wasn't the first time God used the word QUM, however. Turn back in your
workbooks to Day 1, when I asked you to circle the bolded words in **Genesis
13:14-17**.

Can you guess where I am going next? That's right, sisters. Where you circled *get
up*, God used the Hebrew word QUM. Read through **Genesis 13:14-17** again.

When God told Abraham to get up, what else did he mention in that same verse? _
_____

That's right! Both times God uses the Hebrew word, QUM, to instruct his people
to *get up* or *get ready*, He is preparing them for **Promised Land living**!

WHEN GOD CALLS YOU TO A BATTLE, HE EQUIPS YOU WITH EVERYTHING YOU NEED TO SUSTAIN IT.

Three months after God told me to get ready, I was in the emergency room with two aneurysms. I lost 10% of my kidney tissue. Not long after that, my left carotid artery ruptured. I underwent two precarious surgeries to repair it. I was soon diagnosed with Vascular Ehlers-Danlos Syndrome – a genetic connective tissue disorder that makes my blood vessels, arteries, and organs prone to spontaneous rupture. There is no cure for Vascular Ehlers-Danlos. There is no treatment. There is only a prescription from the doctor to prepare your bucket list and live your life well. The average life-expectancy of someone with VEDS is 50.

Indeed, God wanted me to be ready for something. I am convinced that God led me to Joshua's story as a gracious warning for what was to come. It was the truths I learned in **Joshua 1-5** that helped me stay strong through months of uncertainty.

I recently gave a talk to a local college ministry group about finding the courage to face the unknown. Unbeknownst to me, the leader of the group had entitled my talk "Facing Death with Faith."

I chuckled a little at this – not because it's not true. Every morning I wake up with the awareness that today might be the day God takes me home. I chuckled that *only* because of God's work in my life, I don't feel like I am facing death. I feel like I am facing life. Life to the fullest here on earth and eternal life in heaven. I trust that God's plan for my life is the *best* plan for my life. It's certainly not what I would have wanted, but I refuse to allow the enemy to steal what is left of my life here on earth. I share these things with you only as evidence of God's gracious work in my heart. It is because of His mercy that I have been able to write this paragraph at all.

When we allow God to ready our hearts for the unknown, we welcome the blessings of Promised Land living. We'll look into Promised Land living a little later in our study, but for now, know this: when God calls you to a battle, He equips you with everything you need to sustain it. But the first thing He will ask you to do is *rise*.

Let's close this day out by meditating on what the words *get ready* mean for God's will in your life. Spend some time in prayer asking God to make you ready to rise.

Day Five
TRUE COURAGE

The little girl curled her toes around the concrete edge of the deep end. She looked down into the pool's cool water, deeper than anything she had ever imagined. She looked back at the plastic wading pool where she had been content to play all day until this very moment. Then she looked just ahead of her into her father's eyes where he stayed, tall and steady, arms outstretched and waiting for her to take the leap.

"You won't leave me, will you? You'll stay right there?" she asked.

"No, daughter. I will be right here. I will never leave you and I won't let you down," her father replied. She set her chin and bent her knees. She leaped. She flew. And she landed squarely in the arms of her father.

What lies in your deep end today? True courage has little to do with earthly bravery and everything to do with heavenly focus. Instead of keeping our gaze on the deep end before us or the shallow end behind us, let's keep our gaze steady on our heavenly Father who is always with us. He will never leave you or let you down.

BE STRONG AND COURAGEOUS, FOR YOU WILL DISTRIBUTE THE LAND I SWORE TO THEIR FATHERS TO GIVE THEM AS AN INHERITANCE. ABOVE ALL, BE STRONG AND VERY COURAGEOUS TO CAREFULLY OBSERVE THE WHOLE INSTRUCTION MY SERVANT MOSES COMMANDED YOU. DO NOT TURN FROM IT TO THE RIGHT OR THE LEFT, SO THAT YOU WILL HAVE SUCCESS WHEREVER YOU GO.

JOSHUA 1:6-7

Turn in your Bible to **Joshua 1 and read verses 1-7.**

Be *strong* and *courageous*. When these two words are used together in the Bible, God is often signaling a military battle coming down the road. Joshua heard these two words twice, back to back. And we'll see next week that he is about to hear them again.

You may not be facing a military battle today, but if you're living and breathing on this broken earth, rest assured you *will* face a battle.

List some of the battles you have faced or are facing now:

Sisters, I want you to know this: God is with you. There is nothing in your life that surprises Him. And He does not call you where His feet have not already marched.

But He does call you to be strong and courageous. True courage has little to do with earthly bravery and everything to do with heavenly *focus*.

Read **Joshua 1:7** below and underline the second sentence.

Above all, be strong and very courageous to carefully observe the
whole instruction My servant Moses commanded you. Do not
turn from it to the right or the left, so that you will have success
wherever you go

JOSHUA 1:7

What does God ask Joshua to do in the second sentence? _____
_____

Sometimes, we can lose our focus, can't we? Can you describe a time in your life where you have lost focus? Maybe a time when you have become distracted from your original goal? This can be something at work, in the home, or in something that God was asking you to do.

_____
_____
_____
_____
_____

Were you able to get back on track? If so, how? _____
_____
_____

Now go back to **Joshua 1:7** above and circle what God asks Joshua to carefully observe. Write what he is to observe here: _____

God was asking Joshua to pay careful attention to His Word. If we want to live courageously, we've got to be focused on God's Word.

Sisters, I hope you feel God's pride beaming down on you today. You are doing exactly what God asks of Joshua by staying in the Word! I am so proud of you! But more importantly, so is your Heavenly Father.

GOD DOES NOT CALL YOU WHERE HIS FEET HAVE NOT ALREADY MARCHED.

Before we close the pages on this week, I want to leave you with a little exercise that we'll turn back to throughout the study. In the box to the right under "God's Word," write down any truth or verse that God has pressed particularly hard on your heart this week throughout our study.

Then prayerfully consider anything in your life that may be distracting you from living out the truths in the center box, and write those distractions to the left and the right.

Take your time with this and know that we won't ever discuss this in the group study. This is just between you and God. He will honor your honest heart and He wants to hear from you.

I'm so proud of you! Until next week, know that I am fiercely praying for you!

Carry on, warriors!

Week Two
JOSHUA 1

BE PREPARED AND GET YOURSELF READY, YOU AND ALL YOUR
COMPANY WHO HAVE BEEN MOBILIZED AROUND YOU; YOU
WILL BE THEIR GUARD.

EZEKIEL 38:7

Teaching Session Two
THE RIVER BANK YOU CAN'T SEE

ALL SCRIPTURE IS GOD-BREATHED AND IS USEFUL FOR
TEACHING, REBUKING, CORRECTING AND TRAINING IN
RIGHTEOUSNESS, SO THAT THE SERVANT OF GOD MAY BE
THOROUGHLY **EQUIPPED** FOR EVERY GOOD WORK.

2 TIMOTHY 3:16-17 NIV

exartizo = get ready

The Joshua Diary
HIS PEACE HOVERS

To my brothers down below,

I am watching the sunset on this fourteenth day. It's brilliant up here. If you could count my breaths, then perhaps you would know how many times this horizon has changed before me. Shifting shades in every color but black beckon to be recognized. They refuse to go unnoticed, and rightly so. They are worthy of awe.

Time passes slowly near the top of the mountain. I have marked the days with my staff in the ground, but it does not matter. I could stay in this place forever. I don't know when Moses will return from the cloud. I would not fault him if he never came back.

There is a peace on this place. It's not a peace I have known before. It's the kind of peace that invades the marrow of your soul and settles every furrow on your brow. You may find this hard to believe, but I don't think that fear can exist in the midst of this peace.

There is something more. The cloud hovers, boldly thickening in some places and quietly invading in others. It knows no boundaries, nor does it travel with rules. It demands from us our attention. It demands a response. It demands a step forward into the unknown mist.

It's because of Him, you know. His presence *is* peace but it also compels us to press on. Complacency is not an option. Our Lord requires nothing of us save an obedient heart that is ready for refinement.

The sun is almost gone for today. Whatever lies before us when we walk back down this mountain cannot compare to what I have witnessed here.

Be strong, brothers. Be courageous. His peace hovers.

EXODUS 24

Day One
GATHERING OUR SUPPLIES, PART 1

There are four measures in song where I long to live. It's a basic chord progression, just VI-IV-I-V, if you're familiar with music theory. If you're not, you can hear them in the song *Oceans*, by Hillsong United, just before the bridge, just before the lyrics ask God to lead us to the deep waters.

The chords are simple, but they are built for readiness. For strength. For courage. For lifting your chin and looking steely-eyed into the deep that lies ahead, ready to step toe to water and *trust* completely.

This is where I long to live. When I meet Jesus face to face, I want Him to say "well done, good and faithful servant." That I was obedient to His will. That I fought bravely for His people. I want Him to say that I was *ready*.

If we really want to get ready for whatever this life holds for us, we'll have to go to a place where our trust knows no borders. And the only way to do that is to cling to God's promises.

Refresh your mind on the lessons we studied last week:
- God is a promise-keeper.
- When God makes a promise, He always has a plan.
- Long before God calls you, He prepares you.
- God has designed and equipped you to do a very specific job at a very specific time in a very specific place.
- When God calls you to a battle, He equips you with everything you need to sustain it.
- God does not call you where His feet have not already marched.

Which one of these truths resonated with you the most and why? _____
_____
_____
_____
_____
_____

Now turn in your Bibles to **Joshua 1 and read verses 1-8.**

Today we are going to do some investigative work into God's Word. There are seven promises tucked into these first eight verses of Joshua and we are going to find them. We'll play a matching game first. Match the verses in the left column with the promises in the right column. Note: some verses hold more than one promise, and they are duplicated below in those instances.

JOSHUA 1:2, 4 NIV
Moses my servant is dead. Now then, you and all these people, get ready to cross the Jordan River into the land I am about to give to them—to the Israelites.

Your territory will extend from the desert to Lebanon, and from the great river, the Euphrates--all the Hittite country--to the Mediterranean Sea in the west.

JOSHUA 1:3
I have given you every place where the sole of your foot treads, just as I promised Moses.

JOSHUA 1:5
No one will be able to stand against you as long as you live. I will be with you, just as I was with Moses. I will not leave you or forsake you.

JOSHUA 1:5
No one will be able to stand against you as long as you live. I will be with you, just as I was with Moses. I will not leave you or forsake you.

JOSHUA 1:6
Be strong and courageous, for you will distribute the land I swore to their fathers to give them as an inheritance.

JOSHUA 1:6
Be strong and courageous, for you will distribute the land I swore to their fathers to give them as an inheritance.

JOSHUA 1:7-8
Above all, be strong and very courageous to carefully observe the whole instruction My servant Moses commanded you. Do not turn from it to the right or the left, so that you will have success wherever you go. This book of instruction must not depart from your mouth; you are to recite it day and night so that you may carefully observe everything written in it. For then you will prosper and succeed in whatever you do.

PROMISE
A blessing awaits you and it will be huge.

PROMISE
You are a part of God's plan to bring others to Him and His blessings.

PROMISE
God knows and will give us every footstep along the way.

PROMISE
Your enemies will not defeat you.

PROMISE
God is faithful to keep His promises.

PROMISE
You will be successful and you will prosper.

PROMISE
God will always be with you.

Prayerfully read through the promises found in **Joshua 1:1-8**. Circle the two promises that resound the deepest in your heart today and rewrite them in your own words below. Try to rewrite them using tangible examples from your life.

Here's an example of one of mine:

PROMISE: **Your enemies will not defeat you.**
IN MY OWN WORDS: **Vascular Ehlers-Danlos will not rob me of God's peace.**

Okay, now it's your turn:

PROMISE: _____

_____

IN YOUR OWN WORDS: _____

_____
_____
_____
_____

PROMISE: _____

_____

IN YOUR OWN WORDS: _____

_____
_____
_____
_____

GOD'S WORD IS FULL OF PROMISES FOR US.

Our goal by the end of this study is to be ready warriors who have the courage to face the unknown. The first step in getting ready is to gather our supplies. That's just what we have started to do today.

God's promises will always be the first item on our supply checklist. When all else seems to fail, we can remember that God is a promise-keeper.

One more word before we move on to tomorrow.

Reread **Joshua 1:7-8**.

What promise is found in these two verses? _____

_____
_____

How do you think the world defines prosperity and success?

How do you think the Bible defines prosperity and success?

Hold that thought for a few days. We'll return to it again this week, but not before we continue to gather our supplies tomorrow.

Day Two
GATHERING OUR SUPPLIES, PART 2

I am a list maker. I adore making lists. Just today, I can quickly spot at least seven lists surrounding my computer on my desk. And those only cover my to-do lists that need to be completed this week. Oy.

In my computer files, I've got house-cleaning lists, workflow lists, blog process lists, book-writing lists, and packing lists. I especially adore packing lists. I have packing lists for every type of trip my family has ever taken. Beach trip? Check. Mountain trip? Check. Summer camp trip for my son? Check. Disney trip? Check.

My love of lists leads me to wonder, however...do I make the same lists when God tells me to do something? Can I accurately check off every step it will take to accomplish His will for me? Am I as prepared for His call on my life as I am for a summer trip to the coast?

God's packing list for our lives looks a bit different. It includes not only the things we need to take with us (His promises), but it also includes His commands. If we want to be ready warriors, we've got to be obedient to God's instructions.

Turn in your Bibles to **Joshua 1 and read verses 6-9**.

There are two words that are repeated three times in just these four verses. These two words are used together every time.

I mentioned last week in our homework that when these words are written together in scripture, they are often used in the context of military battle. Our study of **Joshua 1-5** will walk us through a physical battle for the Israelites (the crossing of the Jordan River) but it will stop short of the military battles they will soon face.

Flip ahead in your Bibles to **Joshua 6** and note the heading listed in your Bible for this chapter. Write it here: _____

The conquest of Jericho will be the first of many military battles that Joshua and the Israelites would face as they enter the Promised Land.

Reread **Joshua 1:6-9** below and circle the two words that God uses to edify the Israelites before they move forward. Remember, these two words are repeated three times so circle every time they appear below.

Be strong and courageous, for you will distribute the land I swore to their fathers to give them as an inheritance. Above all, be strong and very courageous to carefully observe the whole instruction My servant Moses commanded you. Do not turn from it to the right or the left, so that you will have success wherever you go. This book of instruction must not depart from your mouth; you are to recite it day and night so that you may carefully observe everything written in it. For then you will prosper and succeed in whatever you do. Haven't I commanded you: be strong and courageous? Do not be afraid or discouraged, for the LORD your God is with you wherever you go.

JOSHUA 1:6-9

What two words did you circle? _____ and _____

This is God's first command to the Israelites and obviously, it's an important one:

COMMAND 1: BE STRONG AND COURAGEOUS.

Do you think there is a difference between strength and courage? If so, explain why here.

List some areas in your life where God might be calling you to be strong:

List some areas in your life where God might be calling you to be courageous.

Okay, hang with me because we're about to do some flipping back and forth through our workbook. It might be helpful to place a post-it note or bookmark on this page and one also on Day 5 of Week 1.

Now, turn back to Day 5 of Week 1 in your workbook. Note what God asks Joshua to do in the second sentence of **Joshua 1:7**.

Underline this same sentence in the passage of **Joshua 1:6-9** above on page 49.

This brings us to God's second commandment to the Israelites:

COMMAND 2: STAY FOCUSED.

Flip back to the very end of Week 1, where we listed anything to the left and right that might be distracting us from God's Word. Reread your list and prayerfully consider it. How have you done with your distractions this week? Do you need to add anything to the left or the right? Do you need to add anything to God's Word in the center?

Well done, good and faithful servant. Can you hear it?

Now, read through the different translations of **Joshua 1:8** below and note the portions in bold.

NEW INTERNATIONAL VERSION

Keep this Book of the Law always on your lips; **meditate on it day and night**, so that you may be careful to do everything written in it. Then you will be prosperous and successful.

NEW KING JAMES VERSION

This Book of the Law shall not depart from your mouth, but you shall **meditate in it day and night**, that you may observe to do according to all that is written in it. For then you will make your way prosperous, and then you will have good success.

NEW LIVING TRANSLATION

Study this Book of Instruction continually. **Meditate on it day and night** so you will be sure to obey everything written in it. Only then will you prosper and succeed in all you do.

This book of instruction must not depart from your mouth; you are to **recite it day and night** so that you may carefully observe everything written in it. For then you will prosper and succeed in whatever you do.

How does the Holman Christian Standard Bible render the bolded portion of **Joshua 1:8**? _____

What word do the other translations use in the bolded portion? _____

Glance back at the full passage of **Joshua 1:6-9** above in your workbook and draw a square around this section of the passage. (Hint: it's in the Holman Christian Standard translation.)

This brings us to God's third command to the Israelites:

COMMAND 3: MEDITATE ON GOD'S WORD.

Meditation is a buzz word in our culture right now. Modern scientific data is busting at the seams with the newly discovered benefits of meditation and perks of mindfulness.

But many fail to realize that meditation is a Biblical concept. (I love it when modern science catches up to Biblical truth, don't you?) However, there is a notable and very important difference between Biblical meditation and the types of meditation touted today.

Biblical Meditation is not about emptying our minds, but about filling them with the truth. The world says we must empty our minds to find peace. God's Word says we must fill them with truth.

Look back at the Holman Christian Standard translation of **Joshua 1:8** above. How are we to meditate on God's Word? _____

_____

WE MUST FILL OUR MINDS WITH GOD'S TRUTH TO FILL OUR HEARTS WITH PEACE.

Let's end this day by meditating on God's Word. Choose a verse from **Joshua 1:1-8** to recite over and over again as you go throughout this week.

Write your chosen verse here:

Day Three
THE SIX P'S OF GOD'S PRESENCE

I turned to the left and then to the right. I looked behind me and as far out in front of me as I could see. Round and round I turned, but it made no difference. Everything looked the same. Crunchy leaves covered the ground below and almost barren trees towered all around above. There was nothing remotely familiar for as far as I could see.

We were lost.

We had only meant to explore the woods just behind the hunting lodge. But ten-year old girls are prone to wander, especially if they are dreamers like myself and my friend, Renee. She had invited me to spend a weekend in the wilderness at her family's cabin near the lodge. By the time we realized we were lost, we weren't sure if we had drifted into hunting territory or not, but we knew that we were not safe.

Renee took my hand and whispered, "at least we're here together. I promise I won't leave you." I squeezed her hand in response, but it was a timid squeeze. Her comforting promise didn't comfort me at all. At that moment, I didn't care if I was in the presence of every person on the planet. My problem wasn't that I felt alone; my problem was that I was lost in a potentially dangerous area and I had no idea how to find my way home. I didn't want someone to assure me that they were with me. I wanted someone to get me out of the woods.

If I am honest with myself, I have felt this way towards God before. I am not ashamed to admit that when faced with hardship, I'd rather He just make it go away instead of hold my hand through it. But God knows that we wouldn't experience the fullness of His character if He simply wiped away the challenges that lie ahead.

If we want to claim victory over our problems, we've got to cling to God's presence.

HAVEN'T I COMMANDED YOU: BE STRONG AND COURAGEOUS? DO NOT BE
AFRAID OR DISCOURAGED, FOR THE LORD YOUR GOD IS WITH YOU
WHEREVER YOU GO.

JOSHUA 1:9

Turn in your Bibles to **Joshua 1 and read verse 9**.

Tasked with the incredible challenge of shepherding the Israelites across a
flooding Jordan River, Joshua never wavered. When God promised that He would
be with them, Joshua didn't respond with a shaky hand squeeze for his weary
people. He knew what God was offering when He promised His presence.

God laid out His promises and His commands, and then His final instruction in
Joshua 1:9. Read **Joshua 1:10-11** and write Joshua's response in your own words
here: _____
_____
_____
_____
_____

Get ready. Let's do this. God has our backs. It's time to rise up. This was
Joshua's response.

What was it Joshua fully understood about God's presence that drove him to
brazenly move forward against seemingly insurmountable odds? Leading
hundreds of thousands of Israelites through a dense jungle to cross a flooding
Jordan that raged up to 40 miles per hour at a mile wide after the winter rains?

Surely he had the right to be anxious. Surely he had the right to be scared. And
still, his response was to immediately get ready for the challenging task that lay
before them. He knew God's *presence* was all that he needed to get to the other
side.

IF WE WANT TO CLAIM VICTORY OVER OUR PROBLEMS, WE'VE GOT TO CLING TO GOD'S PRESENCE.

I think what Joshua knew can be summed up with the **Six P's of God's Presence**.
Together, we are going to find them today.

Okay, let's start with a little fill in the blank exercise:

When God promises to be with us, His presence includes:

1. His p __ __ __
2. His p __ __ __ __ __ __ __ __ __
3. His p __ __ __ __ __ __ __ __
4. His p __ __ __ __
5. His p __ __ __ __
6. His p __ __ __ __

Read the verses below in your Bible and fill in the blanks above with the corresponding "P" included with God's presence. Challenge yourself to find the "P" by reading its verse first, and then reading the hint below it.

NUMBER 1 - JEREMIAH 29:11

> HINT: God has had a plan for this world since He created it. You are a part of that plan and He has plans for you.

NUMBER 2 – GENESIS 28:15

> HINT: Because He is always with us, He is also always watching over us. We have a constant, mighty protector.

NUMBER 3 – PHILIPPIANS 4:19

> HINT: God is aware of all of our needs and He promises to fulfill them. He is the ultimate provider.

NUMBER 4 – ISAIAH 54:10

> HINT: God's peace enables us to meet the challenges of this world without fear or anxiety. His peace is always available to us.

NUMBER 5 – EPHESIANS 1:19-20

> HINT: Our God created the world and conquered death. That same power lives in us.

NUMBER 6 – 2 CORINTHIANS 4:7-10

> HINT: Most importantly, we have the greatest treasure with us at all times: Jesus in our hearts. Our relationship with Jesus is the most valuable prize we will ever receive.

God's plan, protection, provision, peace, power, and prize: God's presence includes all these things. But the beauty of God's presence is not just that we have these six P's to cling to. The beauty is also that God *does* know the way home. He knows how to get us out of the woods. He knows how to get us to the other side of our flooding Jordans.

Our job is simply to cling to the promise of His presence.

Which "P" of God's presence do you need most today? Remember that God is a promise-keeper. He won't fail you in your need.

To close out our day today, write a prayer to Him below expressing which "P" you need the most. We won't share this in the group study. This is just between you and God. Soak up His presence as you pour your heart out to Him.

_____
_____
_____
_____
_____
_____
_____
_____
_____
_____
_____
_____
_____
_____
_____
_____
_____
_____
_____
_____
_____
_____
_____
_____
_____
_____

Day Four
GET YOUR PROVISIONS READY

When I was a little girl, my grandfather taught me how to fish. He had a small pond hidden among the tallest pine trees a seven-year old country girl could imagine. Under the shade of those trees I caught my fair share of brim and bass, and a few curious turtles here and there also.

I always used a cane pole. I had no interest in (or coordination for) a rod and reel, so the cane pole was the only tool I ever learned to use. My grandfather's tool *box*, however, was filled with an assortment of supplies and materials necessary for a successful and perfectly lazy afternoon on the pond.

Earthworms, crickets, fake worms, lures, hand towels, extra fishing wire, scissors, pliers, small hooks, medium hooks, and large hooks. We even had hooks with the barbs sanded down so we didn't hurt the fish and could throw them back once they were caught. His toolbox had all the supplies we needed to be ready for a day of fishing.

God's commandment to get ready isn't all that different from my grandfather's toolbox. We just have to gather the right supplies.

GO THROUGH THE CAMP AND TELL THE PEOPLE, "GET PROVISIONS READY FOR YOURSELVES, FOR WITHIN THREE DAYS YOU WILL BE CROSSING THE JORDAN TO GO IN AND TAKE POSSESSION OF THE LAND THE LORD YOUR GOD IS GIVING YOU TO INHERIT."

JOSHUA 1:11

Yesterday, we looked briefly at Joshua's response to God's commands. Let's take another look at it today.

Turn in your Bibles to **Joshua 1 and read 10-11**.

What did Joshua command his officers to do in verse 11? _____
_____
_____

Go back and reread **Joshua 1:2** where God told Joshua to get ready. Why do you think Joshua responded the way he did in **Joshua 1:10-11**? _____

_____

_____

_____

_____

What might this suggest about Joshua's character? _____

_____

_____

_____

What might this suggest about Joshua's faith in God? _____

_____

_____

_____

Next week, we will look in more detail at one of the ways Joshua chose to prepare his provisions. For now, let's consider the provisions the Israelites would have prepared for the crossing of the Jordan River.

What items would be in their river-crossing-ready toolbox?
In the forty years prior to crossing the Jordan River, God fed the Israelites daily with manna falling from heaven. The Israelites continued to receive manna from heaven during their time at the river bank, but some scholars agree that there would have been an awareness among the Israelites that the provision of manna was about to cease once they entered the bountiful harvest of the Promised Land. It is likely that food preparation equipment would have been found in their toolbox. Clothing, weapons, and military armor would have also been included. Many of their general tools would have been made of bronze, and would have included items such as buckets, horns, and kettles.

These are all very *practical* materials needed for a very *spiritual* battle.

Sometimes, we have to be very practical in our quest for spiritual readiness. So today we are going to consider the practical provisions we might need to heed God's call to be ready.

SPIRITUAL READINESS REQUIRES PRACTICAL PLANNING.

Here's an example: I have several "Code Red" files placed throughout my home and office. If I had you over for coffee and let you peek into my home, you might find a Code Red file in my digital email folders, in my office file cabinet, or in my prayer journal. What would you find in one of my Code Red files? Mementos, cards, words of encouragement, special prayers, and favorite scripture verses...basically anything that would help me move forward and keep my chin up in case of an unusually bad day or difficult season of life. When I feel like I want to quit, I pull out my Code Red file.

What items would be in your ready toolbox?
My Code Red files are just one of the items I place in my ready toolbox. Take a moment and consider the things you might place in yours. I've listed some examples below. Circle the ones that might be useful for you and add some of your own in the margins. Consider not only the items that would encourage you, but also the items that are *absolute requirements* for spiritual readiness.

Your Ready Toolbox

YOUR BIBLE

A WORSHIP CD OR PLAYLIST

YOUR FAVORITE BOOK

A NOTE FROM A FRIEND

YOUR CODE RED FILE

A LIST OF FAVORITE SCRIPTURES

PRAYERS FOR SPECIFIC STRUGGLES

COMFORT FOOD RECIPES

YOUR FAVORITE BIBLE STUDY

SCRIPTURE MEMORY CARDS

A PRAYER JOURNAL

A LIST OF ANSWERED PRAYERS & PRAISES

SOMETHING THAT MAKES YOU SMILE

A BIBLE STUDY JOURNAL

ADD SOME OF YOUR OWN...

One final readiness tool we'll add before we close out this day: people. Friends and family, mentors and pastors. The people in your life have been put there for a reason.

Who are the people in your ready toolbox? Who are the ones you would call on in the midst of hardship and trial?

To close this day, take a few moments to pray for those people in your ready toolbox. If you don't have anyone in your ready toolbox today, ask God to reveal someone in your life who needs a ready friend also. They just might be praying for you too.

One more day for this week! You're doing great! I am praying for you and God is proud of you!

Day Five
TRUE SUCCESS

My son loaded his hockey equipment into the car and climbed in the back seat. I waited for him to buckle his seat belt, my hands twisting on the steering wheel subconsciously. I glanced back at him and casually asked, "How are you doing, bud?" Although, there was nothing casual about my heart at the moment.

His team had lost. Again.

"Fine! What's for dinner?" he replied with a chipper voice. Stunned, I glanced in the rear-view mirror to make sure I had heard him correctly. I had fully expected to pull out all of the *mommy-stops* to ease his disappointment. You know...bake the chocolate chip cookies, promise a movie night with all the popcorn, and give extra snuggles before bed.

To my surprise, none of that would be needed. My son was as happy as a clam. I asked him how he felt about losing another game and this was his reply:

"It's okay, Mom. It's nice to win, but that's not why I play. I play because it's fun."

Well. It seems my son had learned one of the true meanings of success long before I did, at least in the Mini-Mite Hockey world. At the tender age of six, he understood that the world's definition of success was not always the correct one.

I think Joshua would agree.

ABOVE ALL, BE STRONG AND VERY COURAGEOUS TO CAREFULLY OBSERVE THE WHOLE INSTRUCTION MY SERVANT MOSES COMMANDED YOU. DO NOT TURN FROM IT TO THE RIGHT OR THE LEFT, SO THAT YOU WILL HAVE SUCCESS WHEREVER YOU GO. THIS BOOK OF INSTRUCTION MUST NOT DEPART FROM YOUR MOUTH; YOU ARE TO RECITE IT DAY AND NIGHT SO THAT YOU MAY CAREFULLY OBSERVE EVERYTHING WRITTEN IN IT. FOR THEN YOU WILL PROSPER AND SUCCEED IN WHATEVER YOU DO.

JOSHUA 1:7-8

Turn in your Bible to **Joshua 1 and read verses 7-8**.

We've been here before. If you recall, we searched these verses for one of God's promises on Day 1 of this week. Turn back there to find our matching game for finding promises and note the promise found in **Joshua 1:7-8**. Rewrite it here: ____

_____

_____

Now, skim down near the end of Day 1 and review your thoughts on Biblical success verses world success.

In your definitions of prosperity and success, how are the world's definitions different from Biblical definitions? _____

_____

_____

_____

_____

Today we are going to take a closer look at how success was defined in the book of Joshua and in the Bible overall.

Reread **Joshua 1:7-8** and refresh your mind on the three commands from God in this passage (Day 2 of this week).

The Israelites were preparing for a physical battle at the crossing of the Jordan River and an intense military battle through the conquest of the Promised Land. I find it interesting, then, that God's commands to Joshua include nothing of military readiness except for finding strength and courage.

What was success for the Israelites dependent upon? _____

_____

_____

_____

> SUCCESS IS DEPENDENT ON THE PEOPLE'S OBSERVANCE OF THE LAW OF MOSES, NOT BY THEIR MILITARY COMPETENCE.
>
> KENNETH A. MATTHEWS, *JOSHUA*

Do you think our success is dependent on anything different today?_____

_____

_____

_____

_____

Success for the Israelites meant safe entry into the Canaan, the Promised Land. It also meant victory over the enemies they were about to meet in Canaan.

How would you define success for your life today? _____
_____
_____
_____

THE ROAD TO BIBLICAL SUCCESS IS PAVED WITH OBEDIENT HEARTS.

Let's take a look at a few other passages in the Bible to help us round out our understanding of Biblical success. Choose three passages below to read. Note what each passage teaches about success.

1 KINGS 2:1-3

PROVERBS 3:1-4

JOHN 16:33

JAMES 1:2-4

GALATIANS 5:22-23

MATTHEW 16:24-28

MATTHEW 6:19-21

Did what you read in the above verses change your definition of success for your life today? If so, how?

WE CANNOT COMPROMISE ON OUR OBEDIENCE TO THE LORD
AND CONTINUE TO EXPECT HIS FAVOR.

PASTOR DAVID HORNER, *EQUIPPED FOR LIFE*

Okay, sisters. God is ringing bells of delight over you this week. Well done, good and faithful servants! I am praying God's presence would be tangibly felt until our time together next week!

Until then, carry on, warriors!

Week Three

JOSHUA 2

HE HAS PREPARED HIS DEADLY WEAPONS; HE MAKES READY HIS
FLAMING ARROWS.

PSALM 7:13 NIV

Teaching Session Three
A SCARLET CORD FOR ALL

The Joshua Diary
I REMEMBER

I remember the feel of the lamb's coat. It was my responsibility to take care of him until the fourteenth day.

I remember pouring the blood into the basin.

I remember gathering the hyssop from behind the house.

I remember watching the streak of blood as it dried on our doorframe.

I remember helping my father build the roasting fire.

I remember the taste of the bitter herbs and the bread without yeast.

I remember my father reminding me to tuck my cloak into my belt.

I remember making sure my sandals were tied.

I remember watching Elishama hold his staff strong in his hands, ready.

I remember we ate quickly.

I remember not wanting to close my eyes that night.

I remember counting my breaths until the sunrise.

I remember the wailing in the streets.

I remember my mother's voice lifted in praise.

I remember it was the Lord who saved me.

    This I will never forget.

EXODUS 12

Day One
SECOND CHANCES

My heart sank. I had bombed the test.

I had studied the material. I had memorized the key terms. Somehow, my brain just wasn't ready to fully grasp the knowledge needed to pass the test.

I met with my teacher after class. Chemistry was never my specialty. I was only taking the AP course because I needed it to round out my transcript for the college applications I was about to send out.

Thankfully my teacher recognized that my efforts in studying were genuine. I just needed more time. And a second chance.

He worked with me every afternoon for the next week and allowed me to take the test again. I didn't ace it, but I did bring my score up enough to a respectable grade.

My high school chemistry class isn't the only place I've been thankful for second chances. My walk with God is full of moments where I have dropped to my knees in thanksgiving over an opportunity to finally get something right.

God loves to offer do-overs. Just ask Joshua.

Refresh your mind on the lessons we studied last week:

- God's Word is full of promises for us.
- We must fill our minds with God's truth to fill our hearts with peace.
- If we want to claim victory over our problems, we've got to cling to God's presence.
- Spiritual readiness requires practical planning.
- The road to Biblical success is paved with obedient hearts.

Which one of these truths resonated with you the most and why? _____
_____
_____
_____

JOSHUA SON OF NUN **SECRETLY** SENT TWO MEN AS SPIES FROM THE
ACACIA GROVE, SAYING, "GO AND SCOUT THE LAND, ESPECIALLY JERICHO."
SO THEY LEFT, AND THEY CAME TO THE HOUSE OF A WOMAN, A
PROSTITUTE NAMED RAHAB, AND STAYED THERE.

JOSHUA 2:1

Turn in your Bibles to **Joshua 2 and read verse 1.**

That's as far as we are going to get into the second chapter of Joshua today and
I've got just a few questions to go with it.

What did Joshua send the two men to do? _____
_____
_____
_____

And how did he send them? (hint: the adverb here is bolded in **Joshua 2:1** written
above)

Why do you think Joshua would have sent them secretly?

We've got some background reading to do for today so let's go ahead and dive
into it.

Turn in your Bibles to **Numbers and read chapters 13-14.**

In your own words, summarize what happened in each of the chapters from
Numbers below:

NUMBERS 13

What do you think Joshua learned from his first experience as a spy? _____
_____
_____
_____
_____
_____

Now go back and re-read **Joshua 2:1** again. In what way is his decision to send spies into Canaan different from his experience in Numbers?

How do you think Joshua's experience as a spy for Moses affected the decisions he makes as a leader in **Joshua 2:1**?

GOD IS A GOD OF SECOND CHANCES.

Nothing in Joshua's actions from **Numbers 13-14** reflects poor choices or behavior that needs correcting. In fact, Joshua and Caleb are rewarded for their faithfulness by being the only ones from their generation allowed into the Promised Land.

But it is reassuring to know that when God's plan seems to be foiled, He will plan a do-over. In fact, God is about to use Joshua's second chance to give Rahab a second chance of her own.

We'll delve into Rahab's second chance more this week, but to close out today: Can you think of a time in your life that God allowed a second chance? If so, write it here and take a few moments in prayer and thank God for it.

Day Two
WATCH FOR ME

My prayer for the past several months has been two things: that God would flood me with His Holy Spirit and that He would make me fall more and more in love with Jesus every day. Funny thing how God answers prayers sometimes. His answer to this prayer has been to make me want it more. It's not enough. There will never be enough Jesus. I want more.

I got frustrated with this during worship in church recently. It wasn't a frustration born out of disappointment, but rather from impatience. Impatience in the realization that for as many glimpses of heaven that God allows us to see here and now on earth, for as many times as we get to witness His glory in answered prayers and the awareness of His movement, its simply not enough to satiate our deep craving for the Savior of mankind. I want it all. I want it now. I want His kingdom to come now.

Rather than filling my cup, God has made me ready. Anxiously and impatiently ready. It's a sitting-on-the-edge-of-your-seat or standing-on-the-balls-of-your-feet kind of readiness. It's a draw-the-arrow-back-and-keep-the-bow-taut kind of readiness. It's a readiness that's willing to open the door to the doctor's office, dial the number of the estranged family member, or put two feet on the floor on a morning you'd rather stay in bed.

But at the heart of all that readiness is simple and pure hope. What we see here now is just for a little while. The inheritance we are about to receive will never end. Shift forward to the balls of your feet and draw back the arrow. Hope lies on the other side of our readiness.

BUT SHE HAD TAKEN THEM UP TO THE ROOF AND HIDDEN THEM AMONG THE STALKS OF FLAX THAT SHE HAD ARRANGED ON THE ROOF.

JOSHUA 2:6

Turn in your Bibles to **Joshua 2 and read verses 2-7.**

What is the name of the woman in **Joshua 2**? _____

From our teaching session for this week, let's recap some basic facts that we know about Rahab and the city of Jericho:

- Rahab was a Canaanite, a people who were known enemies to the Israelites.
- Rahab lived in Jericho and operated under the authority of the king of Jericho.
- The Canaanites were polytheistic, meaning they worshipped several gods and had no respect for Yahweh, the one true God.
- Rahab was a prostitute.
- If you participated in the teaching session for this week, look back at your notes and jot down any other facts that you learned about Rahab and Jericho here:
-
-
-

Now let's gather some information about Rahab's character that can be gleaned by thinking through her actions in **Joshua 2:2-7**. Reread these verses again and put yourself in Rahab's shoes.

Write a few sentences that might summarize what we know about Rahab's character. I've started you off with a few of mine:

- Rahab was a woman ready to act.
- Rahab was not afraid to put herself in danger if it meant protection for her family.
-
-
-
-
-

I don't think it's reaching very far to assume that Rahab was ready for a new way. Life as a prostitute in the ancient world was not an easy one. Rahab's house was built into the city wall of Jericho (**Joshua 2:15**). It was the perfect spot to serve as a watchtower. She was waiting, ready, and watching for God to move. She was looking for her new way.

IF WE WANT TO BE READY FOR GOD'S PLAN FOR OUR LIFE, WE'VE GOT TO BE WATCHING FOR HIS MOVEMENT.

Ultimately, what Rahab was waiting for was God's movement. As New Testament believers, we are blessed to witness God's mighty hand move in our lives. But ultimately, what *we* are waiting for is the return of Christ.

What words come to mind when you think about Christ's return?

Does it make you anxious or hopeful?

Turn in your Bibles to **Mark 13 and read verses 32-37**.

Based on these verses in **Mark 13**, what kind of attitude are we to have until Christ's return?

What kind of behavior are we to exhibit?

Now read **Luke 12:35-36** below.

Be ready for service and have your lamps lit. You must be like people waiting for their master to return from the wedding banquet so that when he comes and knocks, they can open the door for him at once.

LUKE 12:35-36

How can we be ready for service to our King? Using what we have learned already from the book of Joshua, write three tangible things you can do this week to help you watch for God's movement and be ready for Him:

Day Three
GOD HAS ALWAYS BEEN READY

- The internist that saw me through the first several rounds of tests and was unwilling to accept an easy diagnosis.
- The surgeon that knew immediately that I had Vascular Ehlers-Danlos, before I had been tested and before anyone else had recognized it.
- The nurse that would eventually put me in contact with a local support group for EDS because her best friend also had the disorder.

These are just three small examples of what would appear to be coincidences in our journey toward my official diagnosis of Vascular Ehlers-Danlos Syndrome. But I know better. God was ready for that journey. I know that He purposefully placed these people along our path so that we could easily get the help and care that I needed.

We shouldn't be surprised to learn that God has been getting things ready for us. He has done this all along for His people.

Before He created man and woman, God planted the garden that would feed them. Before He sent the rains to flood the earth, God called forth the first chirp of the dove that would bring Noah a sign of peace. Before He called His people out of Egypt, God called an infant Moses out of the reeds of the Nile. Before Jesus died to promise salvation for all, God watered the tree that would become the cross.

God is preparing things for *you* even now.

WHEN WE HEARD THIS, WE LOST HEART, AND EVERYONE'S COURAGE FAILED BECAUSE OF YOU, FOR THE LORD YOUR GOD IS GOD IN HEAVEN ABOVE AND ON EARTH BELOW.

JOSHUA 2:11

Turn in your Bibles to **Joshua 2 and read verses 8-11.**

In your own words, summarize what Rahab tells the spies in verses 8-11:

If you skip ahead to **Joshua 6**, you'll learn that Rahab's city of Jericho is doomed for destruction. We are going to see tomorrow that God allowed Rahab and her family to be spared from this.

Glancing back at your summary of verses 8-11, why do you think God spared Rahab? _____
_____
_____
_____
_____

God is indeed faithful to all who profess His name. What did Rahab acknowledge in **Joshua 2:11**? _____
_____
_____
_____

Certainly, God spared Rahab's life because she was faithful to Him. But God had yet another purpose in saving Rahab and her family, but to find it we'll have to travel to the New Testament.

The first words of the New Testament begin with a genealogy of Jesus. Read the words of **Matthew 1:5-6** below.

Salmon fathered Boaz by Rahab, Boaz fathered Obed by Ruth,
Obed fathered Jesse, and Jesse fathered King David.

MATTHEW 1:5-6a

Is there anyone in those two verses that you recognize from our story in Joshua? Rahab would become King David's great-great grandmother! And from the lineage of King David would come the Savior of the world, Jesus Christ.

Our ready Rahab is a direct ancestor to our loving Savior. Not a bad plan for a woman who took a leap of faith on a second chance, huh? God can do mighty things with a ready woman, sister. What is He planning for you?

YOUR LIFE IS NOT AN ACCIDENT. GOD HAS BEEN GETTING THINGS READY FOR YOU SINCE THE BEGINNING OF TIME.

Let's take a look at a few verses that help drive this point home. Read through the verses on the left and re-write them in your own words on the right.

HABBAKUK 1:5

JEREMIAH 1:5

EPHESIANS 2:10

JOHN 14:3

1 CORINTHIANS 2:9

Which verse above resonates the most with you today. Why? _____
_____
_____
_____
_____
_____
_____

Before we close out this day, I want to leave you with one more thing that God is preparing. **Isaiah 30** tells of the punishment coming for the King of Assyria, who had long been promoting acts of evil. Read, in particular, **Isaiah 30:33** below:

Indeed! Topheth has been ready for the king for a long time now.
Its funeral pyre is deep and wide, with plenty of fire and wood.
The breath of the LORD, like a torrent of brimstone, kindles it.

ISAIAH 30:33

Not only is God preparing good things for us, but He is preparing punishment for the enemy.

After the recent news of a friend's death due to cancer, this truth is particularly relevant to me this morning. In our broken world, we may often see battles lost to an evil world. But rest assured, faithful warrior, that God will have the last word. We serve a God who is getting a funeral pyre ready for the enemy while He is getting heaven ready for us.

Day Four
THE SHELTER OF THE BLOOD

It was an easy decision to make. In light of all that had happened, securing my salvation felt like the hope I had been waiting for.

I don't remember what the pastor preached on. I barely remember feeling my feet as they surged forward down the aisle. But I do remember every song that was sang that night. God would not be ignored. My heart could not turn away.

It seemed like such an easy fix. Recognizing that I was a sinner and in need of a Savior. Inviting Jesus into my heart. Could it really be that simple? Could God really fill the hole in my twelve-year-old heart left by the recent death of my mother? Could He lead me through this broken world unscathed?

The answers to each of these questions will always be: yes.

And that was my answer when the pastor asked if I was ready to become a Christian.

Are you ready, Heather?
Yes.

One simple word changed the trajectory of the rest of my entire life. It was one simple word that was sheltered by the blood of one mighty Lamb.

"LET IT BE AS YOU SAY," SHE REPLIED, AND SHE SENT THEM AWAY. AFTER THEY HAD GONE, SHE TIED THE SCARLET CORD TO THE WINDOW.

JOSHUA 2:21

Turn in your Bibles to **Joshua 2 and read verses 12-21**.

Today's work may seem tedious to some, but I promise it will be worth it. Hang with me here because we are about to do a little time travelling through the Bible to fully grasp the beautiful imagery in this chapter. We'll start right in Joshua.

What did Rahab ask for in **Joshua 2:12-13?** _____
_____
_____

What oath did the spies give to Rahab in **Joshua 2:14?** _____
_____
_____

What sign did the spies give as guarantee for their oath in **Joshua 2:17-18?** _____
_____
_____

We read yesterday about Rahab's profession of faith in **Joshua 2:8-11.**

Flip forward real quick to **Romans 10:9-10** and write what it tells you about the guarantee of salvation here: _____
_____
_____
_____

The scarlet cord is a figurative representation of Rahab's guarantee of salvation, since we know that she had already professed her faith by mouth. It's hard to read this story in Joshua and not think of another representation of salvation in the Bible.

To find it, let's travel back to Exodus.

Turn in your Bibles to **Exodus 12 and read verses 3, 6-13, and 23.**

What heading does your Bible use to describe this chapter? _____

What animal was each family to use for this first Passover? (**Exodus 12:3**) _____

What were they to do with the blood of the animal? (**Exodus 12:7**) _____
_____

What were they to do with the rest of the animal? (**Exodus 12:8**) _____
_____

How were they to eat it? (**Exodus 12:11**) _____

_____

_____

There was a significance in God's instructions on how the Israelites were to eat the lamb. If you think it's odd that God told them how to dress for the occasion, you might be relieved to know that there was an official purpose here. God was getting them ready for something He knew was coming.

Skip ahead in Exodus and read **Exodus 12:31-32**. What happens in these verses? _

_____

_____

As God was preparing the Israelites for the Passover, He was also preparing them for the Exodus. The Israelites had to be ready for travel.

A cloak tucked into their belt, sandals on their feet, and their staff in their hand would ensure that they would be ready to move when God said GO.

Okay. Glance back at our reading from **Exodus 12**.

What was to happen to the houses without blood? (**Exodus 12:12-13**) _____

_____

_____

_____

What did God use as a sign to know which houses to save? (**Exodus 12:12-13**) ____

_____

_____

What does this remind you of in our reading from **Joshua 2** today?

GOD'S SALVATION IS AVAILABLE FOR ALL WHO BELIEVE HE IS LORD.

Because both of our scripture readings so far today happen in the Old Testament, we must remember that the Israelites then operated under a difference covenant with the Lord than we do now. The Passover ensured the guarantee for their salvation.

But what about us as New Testament believers? We live under a new covenant. Let's flip forward in our Bibles to **1 Corinthians** to take a look at it.

Exodus----------------------------Joshua---------------------------**1 Corinthians**

Turn in your Bibles to **1 Corinthians 5 and read verses 7-8**.

What does this tell us about our salvation as New Testament believers? Who ensures the guarantee of our salvation?

What title is given to Jesus in **1 Corinthians 5:7**?

OPTIONAL: Read and meditate on the following verses that reflect on Christ as our Passover Lamb:

JOHN 1:29

1 PETER 1:19

HEBREWS 4:15

REVELATION 5:6

MARK 14:12

As the first Passover marked the Hebrews' release from Egyptian slavery, so the death of Christ marks our release from the slavery of sin (Romans 8:2). As the first Passover was to be held in remembrance as an annual feast, so Christians are to memorialize the Lord's death in communion until He returns (1 Corinthians 11:26).

The Old Testament Passover lamb, although a reality in that time, was a mere foreshadowing of the better and final Passover Lamb, Jesus Christ. Through His sinless life and sacrificial death, Jesus became the only One capable of giving people a way to escape death and a sure hope of eternal life (1 Peter 1:20-21).

-Got Questions Ministries

Rahab's scarlet cord serves as a foreshadowing of Christ's sacrifice for us and a reminder of the gift of eternal life He brings for all. As we close out today, I encourage you to prayerfully reflect on the moment you gave your heart to Jesus. Take time to thank Him for the gift of salvation and tell Him what you are looking forward to with His return.

Whew, sisters! Today has been a heavy one! I'm so proud of you for getting through all those questions! Only one more day left for this week and I know you can press on!

Carry on, warriors!

Day Five

THE PASSOVER AND THE CROSSOVER

THEY TOLD JOSHUA, "THE LORD HAS HANDED OVER THE ENTIRE LAND TO
US. EVERYONE WHO LIVES IN THE LAND IS ALSO PANICKING BECAUSE OF
US."

JOSHUA 2:24

Turn in your Bibles to **Joshua 2 and read verses 22 – 24.**

Does anything in these verses make you want to pump your fist in the air? If so, explain what and why here: _____

_____

_____

_____

_____

_____

_____

The book of Joshua is full of little nuggets of fist-pumping wisdom. When we tuck their truth into our hearts, they bolster us for the battle ahead and remind us that the Lord is already fighting the battle for us.

WITH GOD, NO ENEMY IS UNDEFEATABLE.

You might have noticed already that there isn't an introductory devotion for today. I'll explain why in a moment.

First, I want you to see a sneak peek into Rahab's life after the Israelites cross the Jordan River. It's another fist-pumping moment.

Flip forward to **Joshua 6 and read verses 22-25.**

What happens to Rahab here? _____

_____

A faithful woman was spared. I don't know about you, but this verse makes me want to clap my hands over and over in praise.

This is what we are after, sisters: clinging to the promise that we will be secure in the midst of arrows flying all around us. I am not naive enough to think that Rahab's journey through the fight for Jericho was easy. But I take great hope in the knowledge that she faithfully hung her scarlet cord out the window and she came through to the other side of the battle unscathed.

We are getting ready to follow the Israelites across the Jordan River next week. No doubt, this will be a difficult battle for the Israelites. I do not know what you are facing today. But I do know that Jesus can carry you through to the other side unscathed.

I don't think it is any coincidence that the stories of Joshua 2 bring to mind images of the Passover just before the Israelites are about to cross the Jordan River. Change is coming for them. But memories of the Passover must precede their battle in the crossover.

Maybe change is coming for you too. Before we face any battle, we must remember what God has done for us already. The quickest way to give ourselves a pre-battle pep talk is to stir up a little fist-pumping knowledge of our own.

This is why there is no introductory devotion for today. You are going to write it for yourself.

No lengthy questions to answer today. Just a vast amount of white space waiting for you to fill it with how God has moved in your life. If writing isn't your thing, no worries. You can make a bullet list. You can draw images of memories. You can write a simple prayer. You can write a song. If writing *is* your thing, you can write a lavish and flowy retelling of answered prayers and rescues made by Jesus Himself.

It doesn't matter how you express it. What matters is that you compile a handful of fist-pumping nuggets that only you can write.... because it's your story.

So now it's your turn. Describe a moment (or several moments) that God fought and won the battle for you.

ASCRIBE TO YAHWEH THE GLORY DUE HIS NAME; WORSHIP YAHWEH IN THE SPLENDOR OF HIS HOLINESS.

PSALM 29:2

Okay, sisters. God is so pleased with your faithfulness! How it delights Him to hear your praise for all He has done. Praying for you until our time together next week.

Until then, carry on, warriors!

Week Four
JOSHUA 3

MAY YOUR HAND BE READY TO HELP ME, FOR I HAVE CHOSEN
YOUR PRECEPTS.

PSALM 119:173 NIV

Teaching Session Four
PUT ME ON THE FRONT LINE

The Joshua Diary
CHANGE IS COMING

Sunrise, at the bank of the Jordan River

There is change stirring in the air today, Lord. I can feel it.

The wind blows furiously this way and that; it pays no attention to the rules of the morning, nor does it have any interest in being still or quiet or polite. It is on the move, whether I am ready for it or not.

The water swirls around these rocks as if it wants to lift them from their resting place. It rushes and it roars, determined to be heard. Tranquility will not be found here as long as this river has a voice.

Even this ground does not feel safe. For forty years, we have walked this ground, one foot in front of the other, only to arrive at the doorstep of change. Are we ready? Will the land on the other side feel safe?

When everything around me is swirling, Lord, you know my flesh longs to stand still. To plant my feet on solid ground and dig deep. But I know the ground I feel beneath my feet is just an illusion. It wants to be real and steady and comforting, and maybe it is for some, but not for me.

You are my solid ground, Lord. And You are always on the move.

I've sat in your presence long enough to know when you are up to something. I've been with you in the tent, Lord, be with me in the flood.

Today I will lead your people to this place that is calling out for change. Untether me from this ground, Lord, and give me the courage to step toe to water. Let us not be afraid of it. Let us not fear the flood. Let the backs of our heels rise up from the illusion of this earth and let the swell of this river rush over our feet.

We will follow You into the unknown.

JOSHUA 3:1
EXODUS 33: 7-11

Day One
40 YEARS IN THE MAKING

"Today, we throw hope in the trash. We don't hope. We know."

I didn't correct her as she wrote my name wrong on my nametag. It didn't matter much to me so I didn't want to bother her with it. Her voice was quiet, but her words were confident. I watched her eyes twinkle as we strangers had a conversation that could have only been scripted by the Holy Spirit.

Her name was Marvella. She was the receptionist for the corporate office where my meeting was to be held. I've only had a few conversations in my life like the one with Marvella and quite frankly, I wouldn't believe all the details of it myself if I had not been the one actually having it.

We had just a few minutes together; but we spoke things over each other that we could have never known about the other person, except that the Spirit of God was stirring our voices to speak words of truth that needed to be heard.

There are many things I will always remember from that conversation, and one of them is this: Marvella had been praying for something for over twenty years. She confessed that the weariness of uttering an earnest and seemingly unanswered prayer for that long had caused her to wander away from God. But during our conversation she renewed her faith in Him and decided to return to her Bible study group that night. She sealed her decision with the words from the quote above. She didn't hope, she *knew* that God would answer her prayer one day, even if not today.

I'm not here to bash hope. It has its rightful place and purpose among believers. But I wonder what would happen if we embraced a little of Marvella's attitude and skipped right over hoping to knowing. There is a distinct difference between the two.

God's faithfulness is worthy of our absolutes. If you've been waiting for a response from Him for a while, you can trust Him to come through.

Refresh your mind on the lessons we studied last week:

- God is a God of second chances.
- If we want to be ready for God's plan for our life, we've got to be watching for His movement.
- Your life is not an accident, God has been getting things ready for you since the beginning of time.
- God's salvation is available for all who believe He is Lord.
- With God, no enemy is undefeatable.

Which one of these truths resonated with you the most and why? _____
_____
_____
_____

JOSHUA STARTED EARLY THE NEXT MORNING AND LEFT THE ACACIA GROVE WITH ALL THE ISRAELITES. THEY WENT AS FAR AS THE JORDAN AND STAYED THERE BEFORE CROSSING.

JOSHUA 3:1

Turn in your Bibles to **Joshua 3 and read verse 1.**

Well, just like day one of last week, one verse in is as far as we are going to get into the third chapter of Joshua today. Clearly, I've got nothing against a snail's pace!

This one verse always gives me pause. Within the grand scheme of things in the Christian community, it's not a verse that comes to mind as an overly quoted verse. I've never read a thoughtful devotion based on it. It's a verse that would likely be read and glossed over during a sermon on Joshua 3, in order to get to the "real" meat of the scripture in this chapter.

But there's something about **Joshua 3:1** that always makes me stop and read it again and just sit with it. What captures my attention most with this verse are not the words that are spoken in it, but rather the ones that are inferred between the lines.

In between just twenty-seven words, you can see the Israelites stuck between what *was* and what *is* about to come. They are on the cusp of something new, and you can feel the weight of the past forty years in their hearts as they pack up their belongings to travel to the bank of the Jordan River. You can sense Joshua's readiness as he gets an early start in the morning. You can imagine the anxiety God's people might have felt as they watched the flooding Jordan, but you can also feel the joy bubbling up as they wonder what kind of blessings lie ahead for them in the Promised Land.

Reread **Joshua 3:1** and list a few things you think the Israelites might have been thinking in those moments.

GOD'S GREATEST LESSONS FOR US ARE MOST OFTEN FOUND IN THE UNKNOWN.

Sometimes, the most beautiful moments with God are held in the tension found in the unknown *in-between*. In between one job and another. In between pregnancy and your first child, or your second or third. In between schools. In between one decision and the next. In between the unanswered prayers. Most of our days are lived in the *in-between*. It's where our faith is built. It's where God teaches us to be absolute in our trust in Him.

If you find yourself in an *in-between* kind of moment today (or if you remember a time when you were in transition from one thing to another), describe it here:

Do you (or did you) have any worries, anxieties, or fears about what lies on the other side of your *in-between* moment?

Okay. Hold those thoughts for a moment as we take a look at something that had to have been in the Israelites' minds as they stood on the bank of the Jordan. We actually don't have to turn very far.... **Joshua 5:6** gives us a perfect summary.

> For the Israelites wandered in the wilderness forty years until all
> the nation's men of war who came out of Egypt had died off
> because they did not obey the LORD. So the LORD vowed never
> to let them see the land He had sworn to their fathers to give us,
> a land flowing with milk and honey.
>
> JOSHUA 5:6

How long did the Israelites wander in the wilderness before reaching the
Promised Land? _____

And what happened to the older generation of wilderness wanderers over the
course of 40 years? _____
_____
_____

Why were they not allowed entry into the Promised Land? _____
_____
_____

Spiritual readiness is about **obedience** as much as it is about courage. If you think
back to Day 5 of Week 2, you'll remember that the road to Biblical success is
paved with obedient hearts. Obedient hearts are faithful in prayer.

Read **Romans 12:12** below and circle what it says about prayer.

> Rejoice in hope; be patient in affliction; be persistent in prayer.
>
> ROMANS 12:12

Take some time to think about the prayer requests that you have lifted up to God,
now and in the past. As they come to mind, write them to the right of each time
frame below.

Is there a prayer that you have been praying for...

A few days?

A week?

A month?

A year?

1-5 years?

6-20 years?

21-40 years?

The Israelites journey was 40 years in the making. If you remember from Day 1 of Week 1, the Israelites journey *actually* started in 2091 BC and they did not cross the Jordan until around 1406 BC. So, it would be reasonable to say that from God's original promise to their actual stepping into the waters, it really took them 685 years to make their way to the banks of the Jordan River. That's a lot of time, sisters.

Turn in your Bibles to **Psalm 17:6-7** and write what it says here:

I particularly like the NLT translation of these two verses:

I am praying to you because I **know** you will answer, O God. Bend down and listen as I pray. Show me your unfailing love in wonderful ways. By your mighty power you rescue those who seek refuge from their enemies.

PSALM 17:6-7 NLT

Circle the bolded word in the first sentence from **Psalm 17:6-7** above.

If you glance back at Marvella's quote from the devotion for today, I can imagine that she had this verse in mind when she said it. Sisters, today let's throw hope in the trash. Let's *know* that in the midst of our waiting, in our *in-between* moments, in the unknown, God *will* answer our prayers. Each of the prayer requests you listed on the previous page are safely tucked away into God's plan for you and for those you prayed for.

Let's wrap this day up by writing a prayer that expresses both your concerns from your *in-between* moment and your faith that He will see you to the other side of it. Also, even though you may not be able to see it, thank Him for the work He is doing right now to answer your prayers.

Day Two
THE ARK OF THE COVENANT

When my son was a toddler, he would walk the beach with us by stepping his tiny feet into my husband's footprints. Even when my husband's long legs would take him far ahead of us, my son knew the way because he simply followed his father's footsteps. He never questioned the path before him because he trusted the person who had walked it first.

Thankfully, we serve a God who goes before us in all that we do. There is no need to fear the unknown, because our God has already been there, ordained it, and achieved victory over it. We've said this before in this study, but it's worth saying again: He does not call us into places where His feet have not already marched. Our job is to simply fit our footsteps into His.

Would you allow Him to light the way for your next step today? Even if the path is foreign to you, God has walked it already. He knows the way; all you have to do is follow.

AFTER THREE DAYS THE OFFICERS WENT THROUGH THE CAMP AND COMMANDED THE PEOPLE: "WHEN YOU SEE THE ARK OF THE COVENANT OF THE LORD YOUR GOD CARRIED BY THE LEVITICAL PRIESTS, YOU MUST BREAK CAMP AND FOLLOW IT."

JOSHUA 3:2-3

Turn in your Bibles to **Joshua 3 and read verses 2-3.**

These two verses are where we are going to hover today, but I need you to skim through the whole chapter of **Joshua 3**. We're not actually reading for context and understanding here just yet, so a skim is okay. We're reading for a particular word. Skim **Joshua 3** and look for the word "ARK" or it's third-person counterpart ("IT" as it refers to the ark.) I need you to count two things for me:

- How many times does the word "ARK" appear in **Joshua 3**? _____
- How many times does it's third-person reference "IT" appear? _____

The ark of the covenant is the star of the show in **Joshua 3**. Let's take a look at a few verses from Exodus to discover why.

Read **Exodus 25:8** and **Exodus 25:22**.

Based on the context from these two verses, what do you think the ark of the covenant represents? If you need a hint, turn back to Day 3 of Week 2.

The ark was a concrete sign of **God's presence** to Israel. Examine an illustration of the ark below as you read **Exodus 25:10-22**. Make notes below the illustration about details you find concerning the ark.

Now, let's gather a few more details about the ark before we take a look at why it is the star of the show for **Joshua 3**.

Glance back at **Exodus 25:16**. What was to be kept inside the ark? _____
_____

Flip forward to **Joshua 4:16**. What is the ark called here? _____
_____

Some translations of **Joshua 4:16** use "the ark of the testimony" and some use "the ark of the covenant law" or some variation of that. The reason for this is because the ark was to house the tablets of the testimony revealed to Moses, which included the entire covenant between God and Israelites, as well as the Ten Commandments.

Flip back to **Numbers 7:89**. How does God use the ark here? _____
_____
_____

Now flip back to **Exodus 26:34** to discover where the ark was to be kept, and note it here. _____
_____

Because the ark represents God's presence, let's remind ourselves what God's presence includes. Look back at Day 3 of Week 2 and list the Six P's of God's Presence below:

1. _____
2. _____
3. _____
4. _____
5. _____
6. _____

Put yourself in the Israelites shoes for a moment. As they were about to cross the Jordan River, which one of the six P's of God's Presence do you think would resonate the most with them and why?

Studying the ark of the covenant is fascinating. It tells us of God's detailed plan to provide His presence for the Israelites, it reflects His perfect holiness, and it foreshadows the atonement offering to come for all with Jesus' death. But it is important to remember that as New Testament believers, we live under a new covenant with God. His presence among us is not dependent upon an ark made of acacia wood.

Read **1 Corinthians 3:16**. Where does God's presence dwell? _____
_____

In **Joshua 3:3**, what were the Israelites to do when they saw the ark of the covenant? _____

The Israelite's job can be summed up in five words:

WHEN GOD MOVES, WE FOLLOW.

Today, we are given the same job: follow God. We do not follow an ark, but instead we follow our living Savior, Jesus Christ. Consider the verses below and in your own words, write what each verse says about following Jesus.

MATTHEW 4:19

MATTHEW 16:24

JOHN 8:12

JOHN 10:27

JOHN 14:15

1 CORINTHIANS 11:1

1 PETER 2:21

Sisters, we have the presence of God in our very hearts and His voice in the Word that is open before us. Let's open our hearts to watch for Him and open our ears to hear Him so that when He moves, we can be ready to follow.

Can you hear Him? Is God calling you to follow Him in a specific way today? If so, write it here:

Now, choose one of the verses from the New Testament readings on the previous page about following Jesus – pick one that speaks directly into what you are hearing from God right now. We'll close out today by spending a few moments in prayer over that verse and God's calling to you.

Day Three
UNCHARTED TERRITORY

I had not been this way before.

My job had changed. My expectations for the future had changed. What I knew about my health had changed. After my diagnosis, everything changed.

The hardest part of processing all of this was knowing that I could never return to what was *before*. A very distinct line in the sand had been drawn in my life and I was now on the side of it that was completely foreign, with no way to get back across to the other side. I so badly wanted to go back to the safe side, to the way things had been before. That side was comforting because for the most part, it was all *known*. The illusion of control felt easier to manage because I thought I knew what to expect out of life.

But here's the thing that God is teaching me about the safe side: it's *really* boring. Hear me saying that with as much compassion in my voice as you can imagine because it's true. I know how hard it is to leave the safe side. But I also know this: whenever I allow my fleshly will to control things, God's will isn't being glorified. And that's a very unsafe way to live. I am learning to appreciate the paradox that exists in the Christian faith: that God's way is not the safe way, and yet it is still the safest place you will ever know.

To willingly step out of your comfort zone and walk into uncharted territory with God will require great courage.

But I know you can do it, because I know our God. And He's all you need to know when you find yourself walking a new way.

THEN YOU WILL KNOW WHICH WAY TO GO, SINCE YOU HAVE NEVER BEEN THIS WAY BEFORE. BUT KEEP A DISTANCE OF ABOUT TWO THOUSAND CUBITS BETWEEN YOU AND THE ARK; DO NOT GO NEAR IT."

JOSHUA 3:4 NIV

Turn in your Bibles to **Joshua 3 verses 1-4.**

Okay, gals. Pop quiz!

What is the goal of our Ready study?

If you answered something like "getting ready so we can find the courage to face the unknown" then you would receive a lollipop from me today! These first five chapters of Joshua hold the truths to finding our way and moving forward in God's will, even when we don't know the way.

If there is one verse that drives this point home the most, it is **Joshua 3:4.** Read it again and write it in your own words below.

There is a fear to the unknown. It can be a scary place. Well, scary is too light of a word for it. The unknown can be downright paralyzing.

IF WE WANT TO TAKE THE FEAR OUT OF THE UNKNOWN, WE'VE GOT TO TAKE OUR ATTENTION TO THE KNOWN.

Yesterday we studied a few details about the ark of the covenant. Let's take a closer look at what we know about the ark in this fourth verse of **Joshua 3.**

Reread **Joshua 3:3-4.**

How were the Israelites to know the way in which they should go?

What specific instructions were given about the ark in verse 4?

Why do you think they were told to keep a distance between them and the ark?

The ark travelled about ½ a mile ahead of the Israelites and this was for two very specific reasons:

1. IT ALLOWED FOR A BETTER LINE OF SIGHT FOR THE ISRAELITES, ENABLING THEM TO EASILY FOLLOW GOD'S PRESENCE.

Glance back at your notes from the last page of Day 5 of Week 1. We talked about true courage and about keeping focused on God's Word. You identified anything in your life that may be distracting you from living out the truths in God's Word by writing them to the left and the right.

God specifically intends to travel far ahead of us, and yet He remains with us always. How does this knowledge change or reinforce your confidence in your ability to follow Him?

_____
_____
_____
_____
_____
_____
_____

2. IT ALLOWED THE ISRAELITES' ENEMIES ON THE OTHER SIDE OF THE JORDAN TO SEE THE ARK FIRST. THEIR ENEMIES HAD NO REASON TO FEAR THE RAGAMUFFIN ISRAELITES BUT EVERY REASON TO FEAR **THE GOD OF THE ISRAELITES.**

We saw on Day 1 of this week that the entire generation of original wilderness wanderers had died off by the time the Israelites had reached the banks of the Jordan. The Israelites about to cross the Jordan River were a young people, who had only known a nomadic way of life. They were not equipped for the enemy lines that awaited them across the river. But glance ahead at **Joshua 5:1** to see the enemy's response after the Israelite's crossed the Jordan.

Take a look at your notes from the last page of Week 1, Day 5 again and as you do, remember the truth we learned from **Joshua 2** that is echoed here as we follow the ark: **God intends to and does strike fear into the enemy's heart.** Does this knowledge make it easier to follow any of the truths you wrote under God's Word? _____

_____

_____

_____

_____

What else might be accomplished by having the ark travel so far ahead of the people? _____

_____

_____

_____

_____

_____

_____

_____

_____

_____

When we refuse to let God lead us into the unknown, we miss out on two very important blessings:

1. We miss opportunities to carry out God's will, and thereby receive His favor for our obedience.
2. We miss opportunities to strike fear into the enemy's heart with God's presence.

Not long after I received the diagnosis that would change so many things in my life, I was home alone and heard a giant thud and crash coming from the upstairs bathroom. Not quite strong enough to climb our stairs in an efficient manner as I was still recovering from surgery, I slowly made my way to the second floor to see what had caused such a ruckus.

A framed picture of **Isaiah 30:21** had fallen off the wall; no doubt it had been hanging precariously after my son's latest impromptu basketball practice in the bathroom. I leave this verse here with you now as we begin to close out this day, hoping it will encourage you with the same truth that settled in my heart on the day that I slowly climbed the stairs, in the middle of so many unknowns:

We don't have to know the way to walk forward in God's will. We just have to know Him.

Whether you turn to the right or to the left, your ears will hear a voice behind you, saying, "This is the way; walk in it."

ISAIAH 30:21 NIV

Let's take our attention to the known, sisters. Take a few moments to tell God what you *know* about His character. Choose a few of the verses below to read and note what it tells you about God.

	MY GOD IS....
EXODUS 3:14	
1 SAMUEL 2:2	
PSALM 25:8	
PSALM 99:4	
PSALM 139:7-10	
PSALM 145:17	
PSALM 147:5	
ISAIAH 55:8-9	
JEREMIAH 32:17	
MALACHI 3:6	
ROMANS 8:35-39	
EPHESIANS 2:4	
HEBREWS 13:8	

THIS IS ETERNAL LIFE: THAT THEY MAY KNOW YOU, THE ONLY TRUE GOD, AND THE ONE YOU HAVE SENT—JESUS CHRIST.

JOHN 17:3

Day Four
CONSECRATE YOURSELF

There was a time recently when I was at a loss for words in my prayers. So many loved ones were hurting, struggling, and sitting with hard stuff. I didn't know how to pray for them any harder than I already was and fresh words just didn't seem to come.

Lord, what more can I say to show you my heart for these loved ones?

Show me how your heart feels about me, daughter.

I turned to one of the items in my Ready Toolbox – my favorite worship playlist.

If my neighbors had peeked into my house that afternoon, they would have seen me both down on my knees weeping with tears and up on my feet fist-pumping in the air as I sang my heart out to the God I know.

A lesson was learned that day: When words fail, worship speaks.

JOSHUA TOLD THE PEOPLE, "CONSECRATE YOURSELVES, BECAUSE THE LORD WILL DO WONDERS AMONG YOU TOMORROW." THEN HE SAID TO THE PRIESTS, "TAKE THE ARK OF THE COVENANT AND GO ON AHEAD OF THE PEOPLE." SO THEY CARRIED THE ARK OF THE COVENANT AND WENT AHEAD OF THEM.

JOSHUA 3:5-6

Turn in your Bibles to **Joshua 3 and read verses 5-6.**

The verses we have studied so far in **Joshua 3** have some excellent clues that apply to our goal of getting ready. Let's see if we can find them.

Reread **Joshua 3:1-4** and list the steps that Joshua and the Israelites are taking before they cross the Jordan River (if you need a hint, review our work from Days 1-3 of this week):

We are adding to those steps in today's homework: <u>consecrate yourself</u>.

What do you think of when you hear the word **consecrate**?

Meriam-Webster's Dictionary defines **consecrate** in this way:

DEDICATED TO A SACRED PURPOSE

Have you ever thought of yourself as one who is dedicated to a sacred purpose? If so, describe it here:

Read the following verses and note what each one says about YOU.

JOHN 15:16

2 TIMOTHY 1:9

1 PETER 2:5

1 PETER 2:9

Solely because of the sacrifice Jesus made for us, you and I are holy and chosen, members of a royal priesthood. We have been set apart by God to do His work. There will be many things that God calls us to do in our lifetime here on earth, but our first and foremost job is this: to worship Him.

Take a moment to read **Isaiah 61:1-4**. These were words of prophecy, spoken by Isaiah about the coming Messiah. Jesus Himself would read some of them again at the start of His earthly ministry (see **Luke 4:14-30**). Note what it says about us in **Isaiah 61:3**. What is our ultimate purpose?

I particularly like the HCSB translation of **Isaiah 61:3b**:

And they will be called righteous trees,
planted by the LORD
to glorify Him.

ISAIAH 61:3b

Our ultimate purpose on this earth is to glorify God in all that we do. The traditional view of worship is often seen as singing hymns and praise songs, individually or collectively with the church body. This is, of course, one of the main ways that we can worship the Lord, but there are many others.

Thinking practically here, list several ways that you can worship God:

Reread **Joshua 3:5-6** below and circle the word consecrate.

Joshua told the people, "Consecrate yourselves, because the
LORD will do wonders among you tomorrow." Then he said to
the priests, "Take the ark of the covenant and go on ahead of the
people." So they carried the ark of the covenant and went ahead
of them.

JOSHUA 3:5-6

The Hebrew word for consecrate here is QADASH. It literally means "to be set apart or consecrated," but this word itself is related to the vocabulary of *sanctuary worship*.

Flip back to **Exodus 19:10-11**. What would the act of consecration likely include for the Israelites? _____

_____

_____

Notice the specific word used in **Exodus 19:11**. I've bolded it below:

And the LORD said to Moses, "Go to the people and
consecrate them today and tomorrow. Have them wash their
clothes and **be ready** by the third day, because on that day
the LORD will come down on Mount Sinai in the sight of all the
people.

EXODUS 19:10-11 NIV

The act of consecration, of recognizing their purpose as a holy people to glorify a Holy God, *was done as a preparation for what was to come*. Quite simply, worship made them ready. Flip forward to **Joshua 7:13** and you'll see God command the Israelites to do it again.

WORSHIPFUL HEARTS REMAIN READY TO DO GOD'S WILL.

Because one of our goals for this study is to be ready not only to *defend* against the arrows that will undoubtedly come our way, but also to *offend* the enemy as we serve as arrows for the will of God's kingdom, I want you to see something about our ultimate purpose on earth to worship God and to glorify Him in all that we do.

Read **Psalm 42:5** below and circle the bolded word.

Why am I so depressed? Why this turmoil within me? Put your hope in God, for I will still **praise** Him, my Savior and my God.

PSALM 42:5

In this Psalm, David chooses to praise God, even as he struggles with grief and depression. In this broken world, I doubt you will find it hard to remember a time when you felt like David. If so, describe it here: _____

_____

_____

_____

Now, note the word from **Psalm 42:5** that we circled. What was it? _____

Just as there are many different ways to worship God, there are many different words in the Hebrew language used for praise. The specific word used here in **Psalm 42:5** is YESHUAH, which means *salvation*. If you trace that word back to its root, however, you will find the word YADAH, which means *thanks*.

Offering thanksgiving towards a God who saves is certainly an appropriate response for a worshipful heart.

But if you trace the word YADAH even further, you'll find something more. You will find that its roots lie in the language of the Akkadian people, who were known for their skill in archery.

THE AKKADIANS WERE A POWERFUL WARLIKE PEOPLE. THEIR MOST SKILLED WARRIORS WERE ARCHERS. THE DEVELOPMENT OF ARCHERY CHANGED THE WHOLE PICTURE OF WARFARE DURING THE BRONZE AGE. PRIOR TO THAT THE ONLY WAY TO KILL YOUR OPPONENT WAS IN

HAND TO HAND COMBAT WITH A SWORD. AN ARROW COULD KILL FROM
A DISTANCE, LIKE A FLYING SWORD. YOU DID NOT HAVE TO ENGAGE YOUR
ENEMY PERSON TO PERSON WITH A BOW AND ARROW.

CHAIM BENTORAH, BIBLICAL HEBREW STUDIES

The Akkadian's used the Hebrew word YADAH to refer to the shooting of arrows, which is why the word praise in the Bible can sometimes literally mean *casting arrows*. By commanding us to consecrate ourselves to worship, God is teaching us how to be warriors without us ever having to swing an actual sword.

Sisters, when we praise God we are casting arrows at the enemy. This was one of the last of the instructions given to the Israelites as they prepared to cross the Jordan River.

Consecrate yourselves.

You are a holy people because you serve a holy God.

Cast your arrows and praise Him.

Then watch Him move mightily.

Whatever lies in the unknown before you, there is only one thing left for you to do today. Close this book and worship your heavenly Father. Tomorrow we will see the other side of the Jordan.

Day Five
TOE TO WATER

When I was in college, I was a part of a small group with Intervarsity Christian Fellowship. We studied the Bible together, ate together, fellowshipped together. And we also jumped off cliffs together. One Saturday afternoon trip to the local rock quarry left my stomach in knots, anxious to step off the twenty-foot cliff (forty? I'm terrible with estimating distances), but determined to *not fear*. Everybody else is doing this and I can to, I thought.

I jump. I fly. I hit the water and sink and then shoot to the surface, heaving oxygen and pumping blood. My white teeth shine against the water and I am proud, and also foolish.

Now, as a mother of a boy who is learning to honor God, make good choices, love his friends, and care for his neighbor, I want to live fearlessly for him. What am I teaching him if I am not teaching him to leap boldly into the arms of Jesus? Quietly, I ask Jesus to call me out onto the deep water.

It was a simple prayer. The prayers in my life that God has answered the most loudly have been just that: simple.

Jesus, take me to the place where my trust will have no borders. Take me deeper than my feet could ever wander alone. Increase my faith. I trust you. Whatever you are preparing me for, wherever you are leading me, let me step toe to water and let me keep my eyes on you.

This was my prayer four months before my modern-day Jordan River. These were the words I prayed before I knew what was coming...before all of the unknown...before the aneurisms, before the ruptured carotid artery, before the terminal diagnosis.

No, it has not been easy. But it has been resoundingly *good*. God's plan is *always* good. And so, I whisper often to myself: This is the path. God has a purpose. I will have peace.

What is it that keeps you from stepping out onto the water? There is nothing that God cannot rescue you from. And when you do timidly press one big toe to saving water, be ready for a glorious adventure led by the only One who is capable of keeping you from sinking.

One big toe and a simple prayer are all that is needed.

WHEN THE FEET OF THE PRIESTS WHO CARRY THE ARK OF THE LORD, THE LORD OF ALL THE EARTH, COME TO REST IN THE JORDAN'S WATERS, ITS WATERS WILL BE CUT OFF. THE WATER FLOWING DOWNSTREAM WILL STAND UP IN A MASS.

JOSHUA 3:13

It's here! It's finally here! The moment that we are to watch the Israelites cross the Jordan River has finally arrived!

Turn in your Bibles to **Joshua 3 and read verses 7-17.**

Fording a nation of 600,000 (and that's just the men) across a river...no big deal, right? In our twenty-first century culture, it might be tempting to assume that this would not be so difficult of a task. I know this, because that's what I naively assumed myself.

Allow me to paint a picture of the Jordan River Valley for you. Have you ever been on a river rapids excursion? Okay, put that scene into your mind because that's the image we will build upon.

The Jordan River lies between the Sea of Galilee to the north and the Dead Sea to the south. It sits along a major earthquake fault line between the Arabian and African tectonic plates, so the area itself is naturally unstable. At the time that the Israelites reach the river bank, heavy late winter and early spring rains from the north have swollen its width from an average 100 feet to more than a mile. As you travel southward along the river, its elevation drastically decreases, forming cascading rapids and drops surrounding a plethora of rocks, which were likely deposited there by earlier earthquakes.

Because I'm a visual learner, humor me here for a minute. Taking the details from the paragraph above, sketch the winding Jordan River and anything you've noted above in the box below. Leave room to add a little detail from what we'll learn in a moment.

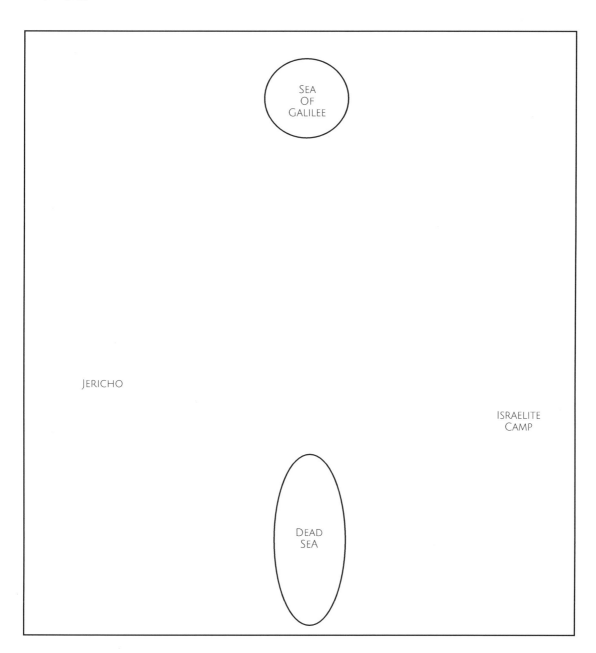

This was not a serene and peaceful river. Take a quick look at **Joshua 3:15** and note what it says about the river: _____

_____

At flood stage, it would have been very dangerous for the Israelites to cross the Jordan. There have even been reports in modern-day times of bathers being swept away there due to the swift current. Add some flooding waters to your drawing above.

Okay, hold that thought because we'll return to **Joshua 3:15** in just a minute.

To even arrive at the river's banks was no easy task. Let's look to scripture to see why. Read the verses below and note how each describes the Jordan River valley to the right.

JEREMIAH 49:19

JEREMIAH 50:44

ZECHARIAH 11:3

To our image of raging, river rapids, we will add what is known as the "zor" of the Jordan. It is the valley's lower level, found on either side of the river. It is full of thistles, vines, thorn bushes, and dense trees and vegetation. Many translations call this the "thicket of the Jordan," and if we want to picture it correctly in our minds we can rightly imagine a jungle. Within the zor, the Israelites would have also encountered lions, wolves, jackals, and a host of other wild animals.

Add these new details to your drawing above.

The crossing of the Jordan was certainly a divine miracle to behold, but the fact that the Israelite nation of men, women, and children even arrived at its banks was a miracle in itself. Weary, travel-worn, grief-stricken and marching into the unknown after witnessing 40 years of loss, the Israelites had to have been ripe for a new way.

Take a moment to consider all that the Israelites had to journey through to get to this moment. Can you think of a time when you have felt a similar way, either now or in the past? If so, describe it here.

Now, glance back at **Joshua 3:15** and read it slowly. How does this verse describe the Jordan again? _____

Now notice what it says about the time of the year. What is happening during this time? _____

Harvest. A harvest was coming for the Israelites. After all that they had been through, the harvest was on its way.

The harvest is often used as a symbol for blessing in the Bible. When I read **Joshua 3:15**, I am reminded of one of my favorite quotes. I heard it in 2002 while listening to Beth Moore teach on the book of Ruth; you can read **Ruth 1:20-22** to see both the loss and the harvest she was referring to then. But I think it's truth is just as applicable for the book of Joshua. Read it below and let it's hope sink in.

THE SEASON OF YOUR GREATEST LOSS IS THE PRECURSOR
TO YOUR GREATEST BLESSING.

BETH MOORE

Sisters, if you are walking through a season of loss, in the thicket of the Jordan and looking ahead at a raging flood, know that your harvest is on its way. You'll remember that this was one of God's promises in **Joshua 1** – a blessing awaits you on the other side.

Write a few words to God here describing how this promise makes you feel: _____

_____
_____
_____
_____
_____
_____
_____

Let's look closely now at how the Israelites moved forward. God had already promised to get them to the other side of the Jordan, but He didn't tell them how.

What did God tell them in **Joshua 3:5**? _____

_____

Let's take our attention to the known here:

- The Israelites *knew* what God has promised.
- The Israelites *knew* that He would do amazing things.

What they didn't know, was *how.*

Is this enough for us? Is it enough to know what God has promised, but not to know how He is going to deliver on that promise? Can we move forward into the unknown *even if* we cannot see His plan? What makes moving forward into the unknown easy for you? What makes it difficult?

We won't share your thoughts in the group, this is just between you and God. But if you'd like to take a stab at answering these questions, write your response here. Take your time. These are not easy questions to answer so be patient with yourself as you respond.

GOD IS FAITHFUL.

I say these three words often. Yes, God is very faithful. But how do we know? The Bible certainly reveals evidence of His faithfulness over and over again. But sometimes, we have to see it for ourselves. We have to live it in our own fleshly bodies and minds and hearts before we can accept it as truth.

God knows this of us. And he knew it of the Israelites.

Read **Joshua 3:8**, **Joshua 3:13**, and **Joshua 3:15**. What do these verses tell us about what God asked the Israelites to do? _____
_____
_____
_____

Step into this one with me, sisters, because this one is a big one.

SOMETIMES, THE ONLY WAY TO KNOW THAT GOD IS FAITHFUL IS TO TAKE A STEP OF FAITH.

From the scriptures, we know that God is good. We know that God is loving. We know that God is merciful. But if we want to know that God is faithful, we've got to move forward into the unknown. Because sometimes God calls us to step into the flood before He will calm the waters.

Toe. To. Water.

It is what God asked of the Israelites. And it is what He asks of us today. Is it time to step into the water, sister? Where is He calling you into the unknown today? God is *ready* to prove Himself faithful.

We will close today's lesson by reading the entire chapter of **Joshua 3** again.

Read it knowing the steps we must take before we reach the flooding river: watching for God's movement, following where He leads, and worshipping His holiness.

> Read it to embrace the courage it will take to step toe to water.

> Read it with the awareness that a blessing is coming when we step out in obedience.

> Read it to rejoice in God's faithfulness as you watch the entire Israelite nation reach the other side.

> Read it as you picture yourself also standing firm on dry ground, on the other side.

Ask God to open your heart and reveal a fresh Word on you today. When you have finished reading **Joshua 3**, note any new insights that come to mind here.

What lies on the other side for you, sisters? God is ready to take you there.

Until next week, carry on warriors.

Week Five
JOSHUA 4

GOD IS OUR REFUGE AND STRENGTH, ALWAYS READY TO HELP
IN TIMES OF TROUBLE.

PSALM 46:1 NLT

Teaching Session Five
TIME TO RISE

The Lord did _____ so that others
may know Him through my story.

The Joshua Diary
I REMAIN, FLOODED

On the other side.

Lord, I marvel at your mercy. Since the last rising of the sun, I have watched my entire people cross from one side of this flooding river to the other. We have made it to your Promised Land. There can be no other explanation for this miracle save the boundless overruns of your grace.

Since the day you called me, many years ago, I have been flooded with your Spirit. Choices have been made with your will at the forethought of my mind. Steps have been taken onto unknown ground with your presence at the core of my heart. When you speak, I listen and move. At least, that is my desire. Lord, let me move with your Spirit!

Today we are flooded with your mercy. Is there anything else in this world that runs so freely and without precept? It seems the only rule that exists within your grace is to expect no rules. It flows where it wants and we either step into it and receive life or we step away from it and....no, I don't want to step away. You are the only way.

We do not deserve this dry ground, and yet you give it to us without question. Why, Father? Why do you choose us over and over again? We have nothing to offer you in exchange for your unfathomable goodness. We are a fickle people. And still, we are hungry for you, starving to hear your voice ringing loudly in our ears, to feel your presence as we move forward in faith, and to see your goodness prevail on this fresh earth.

So we will come to your feet again and again, with nothing to offer, but we will beg for the flood. We will not be content with a drought, Lord. Flood us with your Spirit. Flood us with your mercy. We don't know any other way. We don't want any other way.

We choose to remain, flooded.

NUMBERS 27:18

122

Day One
THE LAND THAT WE ARE PROMISED

We do not enter this world empty-handed.

It would appear that way if you were looking at the swaddled newness of a baby who had taken only a handful of breaths in her mother's arms. But underneath the sweet rolls of baby's fresh skin lie generations of choices, some of them made by mankind and some of them made by God.

Our DNA tells the story of our inheritance. It's the only thing with which we enter this world. But it doesn't have to be the only thing we leave *to* this world.

I remember the moment that I knew my story would be intricately connected with my mother's. Tiny ears, tiny nose, bony hands and a gift for music...these were the things I knew I had inherited from her. I have always sensed that she had given me something else, but God waited until I had settled these lessons from Joshua in my heart before He revealed exactly what it was. True to His gracious nature, He knew I needed to be ready first.

It's a curious process to watch the mind as you sort through the realization that you may share a similar fate as the one who brought you into this world. My mother died at the age of 37 because of Vascular Ehlers-Danlos Syndrome, the genetic disorder that I inherited from her. But as I stand at the edge of my 40th birthday, it's not this inheritance that captivates my mind.

It's the one that I inherited from God when I became His daughter. And unlike the things we may inherit from this broken world, His inheritance is filled with hope.

Refresh your mind on the lessons we studied last week:

- God's greatest lessons for us are most often found in the unknown.
- When God moves, we follow.
- If we want to take the fear out of the unknown, we've got to take our attention to the known.
- Worshipful hearts remain ready for God's will.
- The only way to know that God is faithful is to take a step of faith.

Which one of these truths resonated with you the most and why? _____
_____
_____
_____

AFTER THE ENTIRE NATION HAD FINISHED CROSSING THE JORDAN, THE
LORD SPOKE TO JOSHUA.

JOSHUA 4:1

Turn in your Bibles to **Joshua 4 and read verses 1-3.**

If you participated in the teaching portion for this week, then you'll remember
that the fourth chapter of Joshua is a continuation of the story of the crossing of
the Jordan River. While we saw the details of the *actual crossing* of the river in
Joshua 3, this week we will zoom in on the story a bit more to learn details of the
memorial made to the event in **Joshua 4**.

But.

Before we adjust our lens to zoom in on the memorial, let's widen our lens a bit to
discuss the land that the Israelites now find themselves in.

Having crossed the Jordan River from the west, the Israelites are now in a
territory known by a very specific name. What is the name of the land where the
Israelites are now? (If you need a hint, have a glance at **Numbers 34:29** below). ____

_____

These are the ones the LORD commanded to distribute the
inheritance to the Israelites in the land of Canaan.

NUMBERS 34:29

Ah, Canaan. Also known as The Promised Land or The Land of Milk and Honey.
As you'll remember from Week 1 of our study, it's the land that God promised to
the Israelite nation, through His covenant with Abraham, and it's the land the
Israelites would enter after wandering for forty years in the wilderness.

For the Israelites, the Promised Land was everything the wilderness wasn't. And now it was finally theirs. But as New Testament believers, how do we embrace Promised Land living today?

If you open a late 19th or early 20th century hymnal, you will no doubt find songs that romanticize Canaan as a symbol for what we will experience in heaven when we pass away. It's a lovely sentiment, but unfortunately, it isn't Biblical.

The stories recorded in the book of Joshua detail the blessings of *life* for God's people, not what will happen in their death. And if you read further along in Joshua, you will see the Israelites facing enemies, defeating battles, and struggling with sin. I know you will rejoice with me in the truth that none of these things will take place in heaven.

> THE VICTORIOUS CHRISTIAN LIFE ISN'T A ONCE-FOR-ALL TRIUMPH THAT ENDS ALL OUR PROBLEMS. AS PICTURED BY ISRAEL IN THE BOOK OF JOSHUA, THE VICTORIOUS CHRISTIAN LIFE IS A SERIES OF CONFLICTS AND VICTORIES AS WE DEFEAT ONE ENEMY AFTER ANOTHER AND CLAIM MORE OF OUR INHERITANCE TO THE GLORY OF GOD.
>
> WARREN WIERSBE, *BE STRONG*

The battle and the blessing. These are the hallmarks of the Christian faith. We've spent the past four weeks of this study getting ready for the battle. Now it's time to get ready for the blessing. How do we embrace Promised Land living today?

We can hone in on the ideal of Promised Land living by examining just one word. Read **Joshua 1:6** below and circle the word that is bolded.

> Be strong and courageous, for you will distribute the land I swore to their fathers to give them as an **inheritance**.
>
> JOSHUA 1:6

The word *inheritance* shows up 238 times in the Bible. Forty-nine of those occurrences are found in the book of Joshua. If we want to understand Promised Land living, we'll have to understand our inheritance.

Flip to the New Testament and bookmark the books of Matthew, Ephesians, and Hebrews. We'll be spending some time there today.

Read **Ephesians 3:1-6** and summarize it in your own words below.

Now, rewrite **Ephesians 3:6** word for word here.

Depending on which Bible translation you are reading from, you will have just written one of the following phrases:

> *promise in Christ*
> *promise of blessings because they belong to Christ Jesus*
> *promised by the Messiah*

All of these variations point to the same truth: that because of Jesus, we can claim the inheritance of God. Jesus *is* our Promised Land, sisters.

BECAUSE OF JESUS, WE CAN CLAIM THE RICHES AND THE REST FOUND IN THE INHERITANCE OF GOD.

If we want to be *ready* for Promised Land living here on earth, we'll have to embrace two more words that begin with R - *riches* and *rest*.

Sounds divine, doesn't it? That's because it is.

Let's start by taking a look at why Canaan was so highly desirable from a geographical perspective. Pick one or two of the verses below and note how the Promised Land is described:

DEUTERONOMY 8:8

PSALM 147:14

NUMBERS 14:8

Canaan lies in what we know today as "The Fertile Crescent." It's an area in the Middle East known for abundance, agriculturally speaking. With considerable rainfall and fertile soil, the Promised Land guaranteed bountiful harvests of the most excellent of crops. A word that would aptly describe this region would be *rich*.

Flip back to Ephesians and read **Ephesians 1:1-10**. If there is a heading in your Bible for this passage, write it here: _____

Now read **Ephesians 1:1-10** again and note every word or phrase that resembles or could be similar to the meaning of *rich*. Write what you find in the space below.

Take some time to consider moments in your life that you would define as *rich*. Think beyond financial wealth and contemplate things that you recognize as spiritual blessings. Describe a few of them here.

Now for the times that you just described, can you trace the hand of God in them? If so, take a moment to thank Him for blessing you in these ways.

Now let's consider the *rest.*

Read the verses below detailing the promises of rest that God gave the Israelites along their journey to the Promised Land.

> THEN HE REPLIED (TO MOSES), "MY PRESENCE WILL GO WITH YOU, AND I WILL GIVE YOU REST."
>
> EXODUS 33:14

> REMEMBER WHAT MOSES THE LORD'S SERVANT COMMANDED YOU WHEN HE SAID, "THE LORD YOUR GOD WILL GIVE YOU REST, AND HE WILL GIVE YOU THIS LAND."
>
> JOSHUA 1:13

> SO JOSHUA TOOK THE ENTIRE LAND, IN KEEPING WITH ALL THAT THE LORD HAD TOLD MOSES. JOSHUA THEN GAVE IT AS AN INHERITANCE TO ISRAEL ACCORDING TO THEIR TRIBAL ALLOTMENTS. AFTER THIS, THE LAND HAD REST FROM WAR
>
> JOSHUA 11:23

> THE LORD GAVE THEM REST ON EVERY SIDE ACCORDING TO ALL HE HAD SWORN TO THEIR FATHERS. NONE OF THEIR ENEMIES WERE ABLE TO STAND AGAINST THEM, FOR THE LORD HANDED OVER ALL THEIR ENEMIES TO THEM.
>
> JOSHUA 21:44

Put a star by verse above that resonates with you the most and explain why below.

To close out our day, let's look at the rest that God promises us through Christ.

Read the verses below and define the type of rest described in each passage in your own words to the right.

HEBREWS 4:9-11

MATTHEW 11:28-30

Sisters, are you ready for riches and rest? God is ready to give them to you. We'll finish today with a prayer asking Him to reveal areas of riches and avenues of rest. It's time to take possession of our Promised Land.

Day Two
Heavy Lifting, Easy Stepping

My son has a pretty healthy fear of heights. Recently, he tackled this fear on a two-story climbing adventure at a children's museum. Even with a safety net all around him, he was cautious as he climbed.

"What happens if I fall, Mom?"
"What happens if you don't? The view from the top is pretty incredible."

God does not want us to live in fear. He desires for us to live in freedom. But it's more than His desire for our greater good. God commands us to live with courage. Its not *advice* or an *ask* or a *pretty please, will you be strong*? It's a command. If we want to serve God, we'll have to face our fears.

But here's the good news: once we step into courageous living with Him, the view is pretty incredible. And what seemed scary before becomes insignificant to the adventure that awaits us. That fearful thing you conquered yesterday is the easy thing you'll step over today. And tomorrow? Only God knows, but you can trust Him that He will be with you.

"Mom!!!! You can see for miles up there! See you later! I'm climbing to the top again!"

And again. And again. Be strong. Be courageous. God is with you.

GO ACROSS TO THE ARK OF THE LORD YOUR GOD IN THE MIDDLE OF THE JORDAN. EACH OF YOU LIFT A STONE ONTO HIS SHOULDER, ONE FOR EACH OF THE ISRAELITE TRIBES, SO THAT THIS WILL BE A SIGN AMONG YOU.

JOSHUA 4:5-6A

Turn in your Bibles to **Joshua 4 and read verses 4-7.**

Let's start this day with a list. We have journeyed with the Israelites from one side of the Jordan to another. If your mind is as prone to daydream as much as mine does, or if God has brought to your mind stories of His faithfulness as we've studied together, I imagine that you've often pictured yourself journeying with the Israelites. You've probably thought of your own modern-day Jordan Rivers, and you have praised God for getting you across them.

But I wonder if you've thought of the places on either side of your Jordans: the land that you came from and the land that you now possess, or hope to possess.

Take a few minutes to consider this, then list the wilderness lands that you journeyed from on the left and the promised lands that you entered on the right.

WILDERNESS LANDS

YOUR MODERN-DAY JORDAN RIVER

PROMISED LANDS

Scottish preacher Alexander Whyte once said that "*the victorious Christian life is a series of new beginnings.*"

Do you agree or disagree with that statement? Why?

When I gave my heart to Christ twenty-seven years ago, I naively thought that would be my only new beginning. But the human experience is paved with U-turns. The good news is that when ready warriors move forward with God, each new beginning is easier than the one that came before it.

WHEN YOU STEP INTO COURAGEOUS LIVING WITH GOD, THAT FEARFUL THING YOU CONQUER TODAY IS THE EASY THING YOU'LL STEP OVER TOMORROW.

Reread **Joshua 4:4-7**.

What were the Israelites instructed to lift onto their shoulder in verse 5? _____
_____

What purpose were their lifted stones to serve? (verses 6-7) _____
_____
_____

Therefore these stones will always be a **memorial** for the Israelites.

JOSHUA 4:7b

Circle the bolded word in **Joshua 4:7** above. The Hebrew word used for memorial here is *zikkaron*, which means *memorial* or *remembrance*.

The Israelites were just about to officially enter the Promised Land. List a few reasons why God might have wanted them to pause and pull memorial stones out of the Jordan River?

Consider the moments you wrote to either side of your modern-day Jordan River above. Prayerfully reread **Joshua 4:4-7** and ask God to reveal things that might serve as a sign and a memorial to commemorate each moment that you listed above. These may be events, special days, or specific memories...these are your modern-day memorial stones.

As proper "memorial stones" that align with each moment come to mind, draw them in the Jordan River above where appropriate.

I imagine that the stones the Israelites carried out of the Jordan River were quite heavy. Certainly, we have done some heavy lifting in our lives, haven't we? Some of my stones would have downright impossible to pick up, except for the saving grace of Jesus. But what I want us to see together is that although the lifting may have been heavy, the stepping forward will be easy.

We are building on something with this, sisters, so we are going to leave this for today. But I'll ask that until you return to complete Day 3's assignment, you continue to think on identifying specific memorial stones in your life. We'll return to them soon.

Day Three
RAISE YOUR EBENEZER

We stopped near the top of the mountain. We had followed the winding trail upward for more than an hour, and we both needed to take a break.

"What's that?" I pointed to a stack of rocks that looked more like an abstract work of art than a display of nature.

"It's an Ebenezer," my husband replied.

He went on to tell me that hikers in the area routinely built stacks of rocks to mark places along their path. Sometimes they were used to trace their way back home; sometimes they were used to mark their path in case they became in need of rescue. Either way, they were used as pollution-free *reminders* of something that was important.

The images of the stacked rocks stayed with me as we approached the top. If I built an Ebenezer for the most defining moments in my life, what would it look like?

To be sure, every single one of them would have God's signature.

JOSHUA SET UP THE TWELVE STONES THAT HAD BEEN IN THE MIDDLE OF THE JORDAN AT THE SPOT WHERE THE PRIESTS WHO CARRIED THE ARK OF THE COVENANT HAD STOOD. AND THEY ARE THERE TO THIS DAY.

JOSHUA 4:9 NIV

Turn in your Bibles to **Joshua 4 verses 8-13.**

Okay, gals. Let's play a little game. Can you identify the symbols below just by looking at its visual icon? If you can, go just a step further and briefly answer the questions below each one.

What words or phrases come to mind when you consider this image? _____

What emotions do you feel as you look at this image? _____

What words or phrases come to mind when you consider this image? _____

What emotions do you feel as you look at this image? _____

_____

What words or phrases come to mind when you consider this image? _____

What emotions do you feel as you look at this image? _____

_____

What words or phrases come to mind when you consider this image? _____

What emotions do you feel as you look at this image? _____

Thank you for indulging me with our little game and good job!

Here's why we did that: in our pop culture, symbols are often used to create an emotion or a response. Visual images can be a meaningful way to stir our hearts and help us remember things or events that should never be forgotten. But the power of the visual didn't originate in modern pop culture.

Can you think of other visuals that are used in the Christian faith, other than the cross?

Let's take a look at the visual that the Israelites are creating in **Joshua 4**.

Reread **Joshua 4:8-13**. How did the Israelites build their memorial for the crossing of the Jordan River?

Consider how the New Living Translation renders **Joshua 4:13** below:

These armed men--about 40,000 strong--were ready for battle, and the LORD was with them as they crossed over to the plains of Jericho.

JOSHUA 4:13 NLT

How are the men described in **Joshua 4:13**? _____
_____

The terminology here foreshadows the battles that are to come for the Israelites and it also describes the posture of readiness that we want to emulate. But God's instructions are very clear in **Joshua 4**. Before any movement is made, a memorial must be built. God knew that in the heat of the battle, the human tendency is to forget what He had already done.

Can you think of a time when you lost sight of what God had already done for you? If so, describe it below.

What God asks the Israelites to do in **Joshua 4** is not unlike what Samuel did in **1 Samuel 7:2-13**. Read this story of the Philistines being subdued at Mizpah to discover where the idea of an Ebenezer originated.

Why did Samuel call the stone an "Ebenezer" in verse 12? _____
_____
_____

MEMORIALS TO GOD ARE REMINDERS OF HIS FAITHFULNESS.

Okay, girls, let's do something tangible with this. Sometimes we need a visual to help us remember all that the Lord has done for us. God knew the Israelites would need this, so He asked them to build a memorial. An Ebenezer.

Here's my challenge to you today. Look back at what you wrote down for your memorial stones from Day 2 of this week. Consider gathering physical objects you can place in your homes and in your workplaces to represent the Lord's power, goodness, love, and faithfulness over your life. Is there a visual that you can pair with your memorial stone to help you remember His graciousness?

If you've got a tangible visual in mind, do your best to sketch it here and then answer the questions below about it.

_____

What words or phrases come to mind when you consider this image? _____
_____
What emotions do you feel as you look at this image? _____
_____

Your homework for the rest of today is to build your Ebenezer Memorial. Make a list of tangible items around the rocks drawn below that would serve as visual reminders to the memorial stones you listed from Day 2. Then start gathering your actual items! I've listed a few examples of mine below to get you started.

Before we begin, however, let's discuss a point of clarification. You'll remember that we already built our Ready Toolbox in Week 2. Today's exercise and the Ready Toolbox may seem rather similar, but they serve two different purposes.

The items we listed in our Ready Toolbox are meant to prepare us for the future. But our Ebenezer Memorial helps us to look to the past at what God has already done. **The important thing to remember is that memories of the past can bolster us for the future.** God knew the Israelites would need a reminder of the past to help them take a step into the future. And that's why we are building a memorial of our own today.

Will there be crossover between your Ready Toolbox and your Ebenezer Memorial? Undoubtedly. And that's okay. Once you have it completed, you might even consider adding your Ebenezer Memorial to your Ready Toolbox. I did!

Either way, the goal for today is to gather items that remind you of God's faithfulness that you have already witnessed. We'll continue to build on this concept later this week. Let's remember His faithfulness before we move forward!

My Ebenezer Memorial

SCRIPTURE CARDS   PICTURE OF A SPECIAL MOMENT   HAND-HELD CROSS

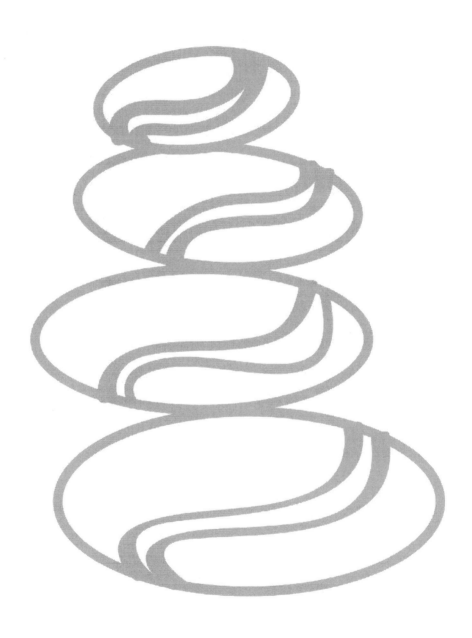

Come Thou Fount

Come thou font of every blessing
Tune my heart to sing thy grace
Streams of mercy never ceasing
Call for songs of loudest praise
Teach me some melodious sonnet
Sung by flaming tongues above
Praise the mount I'm fixed upon it
Mount of thy redeeming love

Here I raise my Ebenezer
Hither by thy help I'm come
And I hope by thy good pleasure
Safely to arrive at home
Jesus sought me when a stranger
Wondering from the fold of God
He, to rescue me from danger
Interposed His precious blood

O to grace how great a debtor
daily I'm constrained to be!
Let thy goodness like a fetter,
bind my wandering heart to thee
Prone to wander Lord I feel it,
prone to leave the God I love
Here's my heart, O take and seal it,
seal it for thy courts above

Day Four
WHISPERS FROM THE SPIRIT

Go help her. Now.

I didn't audibly hear those words, but I did feel a strong tugging in my gut that, if translated, would have said the same thing.

I passed the elderly woman walking through The Dollar Store parking lot as I was walking out. She was moving slowly, with a cane. But my hands were full and I decided I would place my belongings in my car first and then return to open the door for her.

I was too late. I closed the door of my car only to turn and see the woman step up onto the curb and fall, hitting her head on the pavement. I'll spare you the details, but it was a nasty fall. I waited with her until the ambulance arrived and took her to the hospital, all the while mentally kicking myself for not listening to my gut earlier.

I spent the rest of the day knowing that it had been the Holy Spirit trying to move me into action to help that woman. And wondering how many other moments I had missed because I was simply not listening.

Lord, open our ears to hear your whisper.

ON THAT DAY THE LORD EXALTED JOSHUA IN THE SIGHT OF ALL ISRAEL, AND THEY REVERED HIM THROUGHOUT HIS LIFE, AS THEY HAD REVERED MOSES.

JOSHUA 4:14

Turn in your Bibles to **Joshua 4 and read verse 14.**

We are pausing our memorial building today to take a closer look at what I think is one of the most fascinating things about Joshua's story.

If you pay close attention to the details in the fourth chapter of Joshua, you will see the fulfillment of declarations made in the third chapter. **Joshua 4:14** is a prime example of this.

Glance back at **Joshua 3:7** and read what the Lord tells Joshua there. What does He promise Joshua and, more importantly, why does He do it? _____

_____

_____

_____

We have seen over and over again in this study that the presence of the Lord is critical to the success of the Israelites. God's Word makes it clear that the *only* reason they made it across the Jordan River is because the Lord went with them. Take a few minutes to reread the first four chapters of Joshua up to this point and list any verse that mentions the presence of God being with the Israelites:

We've seen in this study that God's presence is the key to our success. And we've also seen that God has been getting things ready for us since the beginning of time. He is intent on equipping us for the unknowns that are to come in our future. We're about to see one of the specific ways in which He equipped Joshua. Spoiler alert: God's presence and our equipping go hand in hand.

Turn back to **Numbers 27:12-23** to read the story of Joshua's commissioning. Long before Joshua stepped foot into the Jordan, God was preparing Him for the task ahead.

Read **Numbers 27:18** below and circle the bolded word.

> The LORD replied to Moses, "Take Joshua son of Nun, a man who has the **Spirit** in him, and lay your hands on him.
>
> NUMBERS 27:18

The Hebrew word used for Spirit here is *ruakh*. It's a word that means *breath, wind, and spirit*, but often, as in **Numbers 27:18**, it's used to refer to God's

143

personal presence. In modern Christianity, we generally refer to God's presence as the Holy Spirit, and God's Word teaches us that the fullness of God exists as the Holy Trinity formed of God the Father, God the Son, and God the Holy Spirit.

But I like this background commentary on the Holy Spirit from the founders of The Bible Project, a non-profit organization committed to exploring the Bible's unified story by focusing on its overarching themes and each book's literary design:

> QUITE OFTEN, PEOPLE ARE INTRODUCED TO THE HOLY SPIRIT UP FRONT AS "THE THIRD PERSON OF THE TRINITY," WITHOUT GRASPING THE BIBLICAL STORYLINE THAT GIVES THIS IDEA ITS PROFOUND MEANING. THE LATER CHRISTIAN CREEDS DO A GREAT JOB OF SUMMARIZING THE BIBLE'S TEACHING ABOUT GOD WITH WORDS LIKE "TRINITY" OR "PERSON." BUT, WE SHOULD BE MINDFUL THAT THESE ARE NOT THE WORDS USED IN THE BIBLE. THIS IS WHY WE STARTED BY EXPLORING THE BIBLICAL WORD FOR SPIRIT (RUAKH), WHOSE PRIMARY MEANING IS "INVISIBLE ENERGY," WHETHER IT'S WIND, BREATH, OR THE PERSONAL PRESENCE OF GOD. IN THE BIBLE, THE PRIMARY THING THE SPIRIT DOES IS CREATE LIFE, AND ENERGIZE AND TRANSFORM PEOPLE. IT'S SIGNIFICANT THAT THE MAIN BIBLICAL WORD ASSOCIATED WITH SPIRIT IS "POWER" (SEE, FOR EXAMPLE, HOW JESUS CALLS THE SPIRIT "POWER" IN LUKE 24:49; SO DOES PAUL IN EPHESIANS 1:17 AND 19).
>
> TIMOTHY MACKIE AND JONATHAN COLLINS, THE BIBLE PROJECT

I find it fascinating that God equipped the man who was to lead the Israelites across the flooding Jordan River by flooding Him with the Spirit of God.

IF WE WANT TO CROSS OUR FLOODING JORDANS, WE'VE GOT TO BE FLOODED WITH THE HOLY SPIRIT.

The Israelite crossing was not the only time the Jordan River was used as the setting for the display of God's power through His Holy Spirit.

Turn to the New Testament to read **Matthew 3:13-17**.

Who came to the Jordan to be baptized? _____

What happened to Him as soon as He came out of the water? _____
_____
_____

Reread **Matthew 3:16** below and circle the bolded word.

After Jesus was baptized, He went up immediately from the
water. The heavens suddenly opened for Him, and He saw the
Spirit of God descending like a dove and coming down on Him.

MATTHEW 3:16

Here, the Greek word used for Spirit is *pneuma*, but it means the exact same thing
as *ruakh – breath, wind, and spirit.*

The start of both Joshua and Jesus' earthly ministries was branded by the Spirit of
God. And if we want to be successful in our callings here on earth, we've got to
learn to be sensitive to its voice.

Flip forward to the gospel of John and read **John 20:19-23**. What does Jesus give
His disciples in verse 22?

Sisters, if you are in Christ, you have also received the gift of the Holy Spirit.
Keeping in mind that the Spirit of God will *never* conflict with the Word of God,
choose two or three verses below about the work of the Holy Spirit. Rewrite each
one in your own words.

JOB 33:4

JOHN 3:6-8

EPHESIANS 5:18

ROMANS 8:2-6

ROMANS 8:26-27

ACTS 20:22-24

If you didn't choose to read **Acts 20:22-24** above, I am leaving Paul's words from it with you here to close out this day, because I think it speaks so tenderly into our goal for our study: finding the courage to face the unknown. Know this today: you do not walk into the unknown alone. Keep stepping, sisters. The Spirit of God is there with you.

And now, compelled by the Spirit, I am going to Jerusalem, not knowing what will happen to me there. I only know that in every city the Holy Spirit warns me that prison and hardships are facing me. However, I consider my life worth nothing to me; my only aim is to finish the race and complete the task the Lord Jesus has given me—the task of testifying to the good news of God's grace.

ACTS 20:22-24 NIV

Day Five
TELL YOUR CHILDREN'S CHILDREN

My soul glorifies the Lord and my spirit rejoices in God my Savior, for He has been mindful of the humble state of his servant. From now on all generations will call me blessed, for the Mighty One has done great things for me – holy is His name. His mercy extends to those who fear him, from generation to generation.

LUKE 1:46-50 NIV

Two years ago, I read the words from Mary's song above and wrote the following prayer in my Bible: *Lord, let my children and their children remember my faith in You and Your goodness, not my sins.*

Rewriting it now, it seems like such a simple prayer. But if you knew the history of some of the choices I had made, you would understand why there are tear stains beside that prayer in my Bible. My rap sheet would make your jaw drop. I have a mile-long list of things I've done that I'd like for *no one* to remember. Maybe you can identify with that sentiment. If you can, you're in good company.

And still, in spite of all of that, God presents a priceless opportunity at our feet: *become a legacy-maker.* He'll be the chain-breaker. We'll be a legacy-maker.

Who does that? What kind of God exchanges destruction for distinction?

The kind of God who floods His people with mercy, from generation to generation.

THIS IS SO THAT ALL THE PEOPLE OF THE EARTH MAY KNOW THAT THE LORD'S HAND IS MIGHTY, AND SO THAT YOU MAY ALWAYS FEAR THE LORD YOUR GOD.

JOSHUA 4:24

Turn in your Bibles to **Joshua 4 and read verses 15-24.**

Sisters, we are going to finish our work on building our memorials today. But before we do, I'd like you to review Days 2 and 3 of this week to remember the symbols and tangible items we have selected to be a part of our memorial to the Lord's faithfulness.

List the item or items you chose to be a part of your memorial here:

Okay, wonderful! Hold that thought.

Now, let's refresh our minds on one of the key words from our study. Turn all the way back to Week 1, Day 4 of our homework where we looked at the original Hebrew word used in **Joshua 1:2** to describe God's instruction to Joshua to *get ready*.

Write that Hebrew word here: _____

Now write the meaning of that word here: _____
_____

Wonderful! Okay, hold *that* thought.

If you could sum up the entire fourth chapter of Joshua using only two words, which words would you choose:

Gosh I wish I could take a sneak peek on your paper to see the words you just wrote! Here are the words I would use:

MEMORIAL AND MERCY

The word *memorial* is all over **Joshua 4**, but the word *mercy* isn't mentioned once. So why would I choose that word to sum up **Joshua 4**? Well, I'll tell you.

It's impossible to read **Joshua 4** and not remember the great mercy of our Heavenly Father. The Israelites were the furthest thing away from a faithful people. One thing they knew how to do well: they knew how to make mistakes. Still, God lavishly covered them with His mercy as He led them to the Promised Land. And He does the same thing for us.

God's call to Joshua in the beginning of all of this was to *get ready*: to *rise*. But when we are flooded with the overwhelming grace of God, the only way to rise up is to bow down.

THE BEST WAY FOR US TO RISE UP IS TO BOW DOWN AT THE THRONE OF GOD'S MERCY.

Therefore let us approach the throne of grace with boldness, so that we may receive mercy and find grace to help us at the proper time.

HEBREWS 4:16

Sisters, I don't know what you have on your heart today. But I know that the Lord is ready to hear it all. Take a few moments to talk to Him. Bring the burdens of your heart to His throne of grace today. If there is something that you need to seek forgiveness for, seek it now. God's mercy flows like a flood. Let Him cover you with it today.

Take a deep breath and feel His forgiveness wash over you. And then glance up at the list of items in your memorial you wrote down at the start of today's assignment.

I have one final question for you today: in your list of memorial items, is there something there that would cause someone else to ask - *what does this mean*? Visual reminders of God's mercy and faithfulness are not just for our edification. Is there something in your list of memorial items that others might see?

I'm going to challenge you to think not just of the tangible visuals that you have created this week, but also of tangible *actions* that you have taken over the past few days. What are you doing that would spark a question from someone who may not know how powerful the Lord really is? From someone who may not even know Jesus?

Read **Joshua 4:21-24** and rewrite it in your own words here: _____
_____
_____
_____
_____
_____
_____
_____
_____
_____
_____

We have an opportunity to be legacy-makers, sisters. Memorials call forth the past only to bring change in the present. But it doesn't stop there. How are you responding to God's mercy in your life? Your choices today will have a lasting impact on future generations.

As daughters of Christ, we are vessels of mercy. How proud He is of your faithfulness this week! He is making you ready today to deliver hope for tomorrow.

Carry on, warriors.

WHAT IF GOD, DESIRING TO SHOW HIS WRATH AND TO MAKE KNOWN HIS POWER, HAS ENDURED WITH MUCH PATIENCE VESSELS OF WRATH PREPARED FOR DESTRUCTION, IN ORDER TO MAKE KNOWN THE RICHES OF HIS GLORY FOR VESSELS OF MERCY, WHICH HE HAS PREPARED BEFOREHAND FOR GLORY—EVEN US WHOM HE HAS CALLED, NOT FROM THE JEWS ONLY BUT ALSO FROM THE GENTILES? AS INDEED HE SAYS IN HOSEA, "THOSE WHO WERE NOT MY PEOPLE I WILL CALL 'MY PEOPLE,' AND HER WHO WAS NOT BELOVED I WILL CALL 'BELOVED.'"

ROMANS 9:22-25 ESV

Week Six

JOSHUA 5

Let us rejoice and be glad and give Him Glory! For the wedding of the Lamb has come and His bride has made herself ready.

REVELATION 19:7 NIV

Teaching Session Six
THE BRIDGE, THE BRIDE, & THE PRIZE

The Joshua Diary
HOSHEA WAS MY NAME

Musings from a 110-year-old servant:

Every day we are faced with choices. From the seemingly insignificant to the noticeably impactful, our life can be summed up with a series of choices. One foot in front of the other, to the left or to the right, sometimes forward and sometimes back, we take an action or an inaction that leads us out of Egypt, through the wilderness, across the river, or into battle. But within each choice lies only two outcomes: one step closer to God or one step away from Him.

A stagnant existence does not exist. We are changed by the choices we make.

It wasn't difficult assuming my new name. One day I was known as Hoshea and the next I was known as Joshua. That kind of change was easy to embrace. The hard part was learning to live it out.

I have been a warrior. I have been a spy. I have been an aide and I have been the leader of a nation. Above all these things, what I want most is to be a servant. How many choices will it take before I reach that goal? And will I know it when I am there?

I don't have an answer for this.

But I do know it cannot be accomplished without falling before the throne of the Lord. I learned this lesson in my first battle. If we want His distinguishing mark to settle over us, our only choice is to rely on Him. And this will change us.

It takes a ready heart to be willing to change. But is this not the goal of a life lived for God? From my first battle to my last, let it be said of me that I was a changed man. I am ready.

Hoshea = salvation. The original name of the son of Nun, afterwards called Joshua

Joshua = Jehovah is his help, or Jehovah the Savior. The son of Nun, of the tribe of Ephraim, the successor of Moses as the leader of Israel. He is called Jehoshua in Numbers 13:16 (KJV A.V.), and Jesus in Act 7:45 and Hebrews 4:8 (KJV R.V., Joshua).

EXODUS 17:8–16
NUMBERS 13:16
JOSHUA 24:29

Day One
CIRCUMCISED HEARTS

"Mommy, do you think that hurts him?"

I continued to whittle away at the mass of clay until recognizable hands and feet began to emerge. We were making a clay dragon together; and what started as an unformed lump was beginning to take shape into a whimsical creature with laughing eyes and a lopsided grin.

As my four-year-old worked on shaping the dragon's wings, his imagination soared. He was concerned that the inanimate dragon would feel physical pain because of our constant molding.

I almost responded with a quick and definitive "of course not!" But memories of my own hardship and suffering came to mind and I thought of dreams that had been laid down and hard lessons that had been learned. I waited until I had finished rounding the dragon's belly before I answered my son.

"Yes. It probably hurts a little bit. But what our friendly dragon doesn't know is how much better he'll be when we are finished. He'll have a bright smile and steady wings. And once he's done baking, he'll be so strong it will be impossible to break him. Now, he's rather fragile and not quite complete."

My son was quiet at this and so was I. Change is hard. Sacrifice is harder. But that's exactly what God asks of us if we want to live for Him.

Refresh your mind on the lessons we studied last week:

- Because of Jesus, we can claim the riches and the rest found in the inheritance of God.
- When you step into courageous living with God, that fearful thing you conquer today is the easy thing you'll step over tomorrow.
- Memorials to God are reminders of His faithfulness.
- If we want to cross our flooding Jordans, we've got to be flooded with the Holy Spirit.
- The best way for us to rise up is to bow down at the throne of God's mercy.

Which one of these truths resonated with you the most and why? _____
_____
_____
_____

AT THAT TIME THE LORD SAID TO JOSHUA, "MAKE FLINT KNIVES AND
CIRCUMCISE THE ISRAELITE MEN AGAIN."

JOSHUA 5:2

Turn in your Bibles to **Joshua 5 and read verses 1-9.**

Over the course of the past five weeks, we have watched the Israelites get their
provisions ready. We've seen them spy on enemy territory, cross over the Jordan
River, and build memorial stones to the God who saved them. One would think it
would be about time that they take a fist-full of fresh dirt from the Promised Land
into their hands, yes?

Well, no.

Two more important events were required of the Israelites to prepare them for
possession of the Promised Land. We'll take a look at one of them today and the
other tomorrow.

But before we do, let's pause for a brief fist-pump of praise.

Read **Joshua 5:1** below and describe the response of the Amorite and Canaanite
kings: _____
_____

Now when all the Amorite kings west of the Jordan and all the
Canaanite kings along the coast heard how the LORD had dried
up the Jordan before the Israelites until they had crossed over,
their hearts melted in fear and they no longer had the courage to
face the Israelites.

JOSHUA 5:1 NIV

Circle the bolded words in **Joshua 5:1** above. The language here indicates fear, of course, but also a loss of will to fight. The Hebrew word used for the verb *melted* is *masas*, and it describes the dissolving of wax.

We can see that same verb *masas*, used in **Psalm 68:2** also so turn there now and read the two verses surrounding it in **Psalm 68:1-3**.

Okay, go with me here for a moment and rewrite **Psalm 68:1** word for word below:

Now circle the first three words that you just wrote (depending on the translation you are reading from, you may only have to circle the first two words.)

I'm guessing you just wrote one of the following phrases:

> May God arise
> Rise up
> God shall arise
> Let God arise
> God arises

I hope you will be as fascinated as I am that the Hebrew word used for *rise/arise* in **Psalm 68:1** is the same word that we saw in the beginning of our study in **Joshua 1:2**: QUM, meaning *to arise or to get ready*.

Because it is such a central verse to our study, rewrite **Joshua 1:2** word for word below:

Sister, reread **Psalm 68:1-3** again and please join me in fist-pumping over the truth that GOD IS READY. He never stands unprepared or unaware of the battle before Him. He stands ready to scatter His enemies while we simply get to rejoice.

How are we to respond to this truth based on **Psalm 68:3**?

If we are going to be worth our salt at all as Christians in this broken world, we've got to embrace the tenacity that comes with knowing this: the sole act of placing our trust in God is enough to put us on the front line.

But.

That tenacity should be bolstered with the joy of knowing that all the time, our God stands on the front line before us...*ready*.

Go ahead. Fist-pump away.

Now, let's return our attention to one of the two remaining requirements of the Israelites.

Re-read **Joshua 5:1-9** and summarize what is happening in your own words.

What is God commanding of the Israelites?

Why must the Jordan River Israelites be circumcised?

Flip back to **Genesis 17:9-14** to discover the origins of this requirement.

For Abraham and for the generations of Israelites that were to follow him, what did circumcision represent?

Read the commentary on the word covenant from Easton's Bible Dictionary below:

COVENANT:

A CONTRACT OR AGREEMENT BETWEEN TWO PARTIES. IN THE OLD TESTAMENT THE HEBREW WORD BERITH IS ALWAYS THUS TRANSLATED. BERITH IS DERIVED FROM A ROOT WHICH MEANS "TO CUT," AND HENCE A COVENANT IS A "CUTTING," WITH REFERENCE TO THE CUTTING OR DIVIDING OF ANIMALS INTO TWO PARTS, AND THE CONTRACTING PARTIES PASSING BETWEEN THEM, IN MAKING A COVENANT.

EASTON'S BIBLE DICTIONARY

What thoughts come to mind as you consider the following?
1. The language behind the Hebrew word for *covenant* implies a cutting.
2. The physical expression of God's covenant with His Old Testament people was circumcision.

Together, we have studied God's promises to the Israelites as they prepare to face the unknown. God offers the same promise to us today; they are a part of His covenant with us. But they come with a cost.

Even the Israelites were aware that the physical act of circumcision symbolized a greater sacrifice. Read **Deuteronomy 30:6**.

What body part is referred to here?

Why does the Lord choose circumcision of the heart as a symbol of His covenant?

THE ONLY WAY TO FULLY LIVE AND LOVE GOD WITH ALL OF OUR HEARTS IS TO CUT OFF ANYTHING THAT SEPARATES US FROM HIM.

Take some time to slowly read through **Colossians 2:9-15**.

I don't know what God has been stirring in your heart as you have progressed through this study. Perhaps He has placed a burden on your heart that something needs to change. Perhaps He has been slowly whittling away at something in you that is keeping you from fully experiencing Promised Land living. Perhaps the cutting away has been quite difficult. Transformative change rarely happens without some measure of pain.

Let me affirm you in the truth that the Promised Land is coming. Whatever you are going through, God has a purpose to it. In God's sovereignty, it could be for any number of reasons, but one of them will always be this one: that you may love Him with all of your heart and that you may live fully in the riches of His promises to you.

But let me also encourage you to sit with the hard stuff. Stay with the cutting away. It's hard, I know. But don't bypass God's blessing because you are afraid of the battle. It's where God will change you.

We'll close out this day with two short questions that I'm certain will not have a simple answer. Think on them anyway. And ask God to reveal His will over the answer and over your life.

IS GOD ASKING YOU TO CUT AWAY SOMETHING IN YOUR LIFE TODAY? IS THERE SOMETHING THAT IS SEPARATING YOU FROM HIM?

Day Two
NO MORE MANNA

I started baking homemade bread about nine years ago. I honestly don't remember what inspired me to start, but I think it began with an unused bread machine I had received as a wedding gift and a fascination with yeast.

Yeast is a living ingredient. It's not like sugar or flour that have no lifespan nor any organic material left within the finished product. Yeast is a living, single-celled organism, a fungus to be exact. I don't know why, but the possibility of making something delicious from something wild intrigued me.

Baking bread requires the same attention to exact measurements as baking anything else does, but you have to know when to adjust those ingredients based on the humidity and temperature in your kitchen. If it's a sweltering summer day in the south, your French loaf won't require as much water. And if it's the dead of winter, you can almost guarantee your bread won't be ready for dinner unless you let it rise near a heat vent. Baking bread is unpredictable and I kind of dig that.

But the main reason I enjoy baking homemade bread is that it takes the one resource that many are not willing to give: *time*.

Good bread is not something that can be done in a jiffy. Trust me, the one-hour quick cycle loaf on that bread machine will *never* be as good as the hand-kneaded batch of dough that you kept in your refrigerator overnight so it could enjoy a slow rise. Yeast doesn't like to be rushed. The best loaves of bread are developed over a long time.

Spiritual readiness, as we are about to see, is no different.

AND THE DAY AFTER THEY ATE FROM THE PRODUCE OF THE LAND, THE MANNA CEASED. SINCE THERE WAS NO MORE MANNA FOR THE ISRAELITES, THEY ATE FROM THE CROPS OF THE LAND OF CANAAN THAT YEAR.

JOSHUA 5:12

Turn in your Bibles to **Joshua 5 and read verses 10-12.**

Today, we are continuing our discussion over the final two requirements of the Israelites before they enjoyed the fruits of the Promised Land. Refresh your memory from what we studied yesterday. What did the Lord require of the Israelites to symbolize His covenant with Him? _____

Re-read **Joshua 5:10** to discover the other requirement. What was it? _____
_____

We've seen this before. Flip back in your workbook to Days 4 & 5 of Week 3. Skim through your notes from those days just to jog your memory on what the Passover meant for the Israelites and what it means for you.

Now, let's zoom our lens in on a detail surrounding the Passover that is directly related to our study on readiness.

The Israelites are having a party. Two parties, actually. You've already noted from **Joshua 5:10** that they were celebrating the Passover. What happened the day after the Passover in **Joshua 5:11**? _____
_____

What two types of food do the Israelites eat in **Joshua 5:11**?

_____   _____

Joshua 5 tells us that the Israelites celebrated the Passover, but it doesn't tell us the official name of the second party they were holding. Flip back to **Exodus 34:18** to learn it's official name and write it here: _____
_____

Now flip just a little further back to **Exodus 12** to learn a little more about why God's people should have a feast over unleavened bread. You'll remember that part of the Passover was about preparing the Israelites for the exodus from Egypt. Read **Exodus 12:31 – 39** to learn about the history behind the Feast of the Unleavened Bread and answer the questions below.

How were they to carry their dough? (verse 34)

Why was their dough without yeast? (verse 39)

Yeast is a leavener, which means it makes bread rise. A good rise makes yummy bread. But yeast takes time to work. If you don't have time to get it ready, you won't be enjoying any yummy bread.

The two most powerful warriors are patience and time.

Leo Tolstoy

I don't know about you, but I am constantly wishing for an extra hour (or two or three!) in a day. But we are allotted just 24 hours in every day, and so we must always make a choice about how we will spend them. Some days, this choice is easier than others and different seasons of life will certainly hold different choices.

There are 24 wedges in the pie chart below. Using either the initial noted or a different color for each category, mark each wedge with how you might spend that hour in a general day. Some days will look different, for sure, so just use an average. Feel free to add your own categories as you need them.

SLEEP = S
WORK = W
HOME CHORES = H
FAMILY TIME = F
CHURCH/PERSONAL TIME WITH GOD/BIBLE STUDY/PRAYER = G

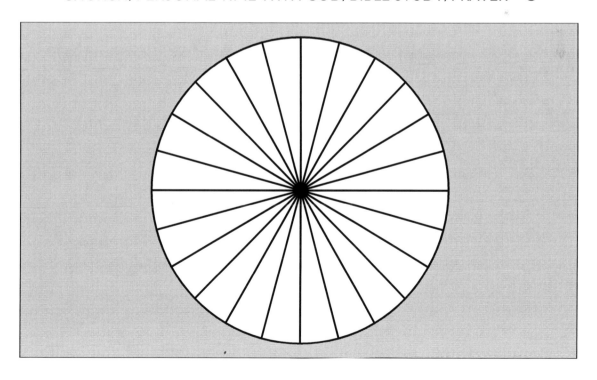

Let me be clear: our pie chart activity is not about encouraging legalism with our time. Different seasons of life call for different levels of commitment towards all things. This is just meant to bring *awareness* to the choices we make on our time in any given day. But if God is making you aware of changes that need to be made in how you spend your time, note it here: _____

_____

_____

_____

_____

_____

_____

It was not long after the Israelites had left Egypt before they began to grumble about their lack of choice foods. Flip ahead to **Exodus 16:1-4** to see how God responded.

How did God provide for the Israelites?

Read **Exodus 16:31** and note what the Israelites called it: _____

The Hebrew word for manna literally means "*what is it?*" I always chuckle when I think of the Israelites looking at the manna covering the ground and wondering just what in the world it was. It's such a perfect picture of the plight of mankind; sometimes we are simply too dense to recognize God's provision for us even when it is staring us in the face.

Can you recall a time when God was providing for one of your needs and you didn't recognize His provision until the need was no longer needed?

GOD'S PROVISION IS ALWAYS THERE, EVEN WHEN WE CAN'T SEE IT.

Can you think of a reason why God would want the Israelites to celebrate both the Passover and the Feast of Unleavened Bread once they entered the Promised Land?

The Feast of Unleavened Bread was celebrated upon entering Canaan so that the Israelites would never forget God's provision for them in the wilderness.

As followers of Christ, we don't have to worry that God will cease to provide manna for us. Read the following passages below and rewrite each of them in your own words to the right.

JOHN 6:30-33

JOHN 6:35

JOHN 6:48-51

Jesus is the bread of life. He is our manna. He is our miracle. But if we want to fully experience the relationship with Jesus that God intended for us, it is going to take time. If you have made it this far into the study, you are well on your way to developing or deepening a solid habit of sacrificing your time. Rejoice in the knowledge that God is so very proud of you! But there's more good news: in exchange for your time with God, you are receiving the greatest prize: a life lived closely with your heavenly Savior.

Before we close out this day, I want you to see one more thing about that feast.

Turn back to **Joshua 5 and read verse 12**. What happened to the manna? _____
_____

What did they eat instead? _____

The diet of manna was no longer necessary because the Israelites were no longer in the wilderness. Now the Israelites must trust in God once again to provide a new way for their sustenance and the same is true for us.

Ready warriors enjoy their fill of Promised Land goodness. Have you noticed the "produce of Canaan" showing up in your own life over the past six weeks we have been studying Joshua together? If so, list a few examples of that here and take a few moments to thank God for them.

Press on, dear sisters. We've got only three days left in our study. Don't let the close of this book signal the end of your pursuit of a relationship with Jesus. He will always be there for you, but He longs for you to reach out to Him.

Will there be sacrifice in the choice to follow Jesus and follow Him closely? Undoubtedly. But there will also be the richest blessing you will ever know. He is our ultimate prize.

> But everything that was a gain to me, I have considered to be a loss because of Christ. More than that, I also consider everything to be a loss in view of the surpassing value of knowing Christ Jesus my Lord. Because of Him I have suffered the loss of all things and consider them filth, so that I may gain Christ and be found in Him, not having a righteousness of my own from the law, but one that is through faith in Christ—the righteousness from God based on faith. My goal is to know Him and the power of His resurrection and the fellowship of His sufferings, being conformed to His death, assuming that I will somehow reach the resurrection from among the dead. Not that I have already reached the goal or am already fully mature, but I make every effort to take hold of it because I also have been taken hold of by Christ Jesus. Brothers, I do not consider myself to have taken hold of it. But one thing I do: Forgetting what is behind and reaching forward to what is ahead, I pursue as my goal the prize promised by God's heavenly call in Christ Jesus.

PHILIPPIANS 3:7-14

Day Three
THE BRIDGE AND THE BRIDE

My fingers were ice cold. One of my bridesmaids covered one of my hands with hers. I smoothed the tulle of my dress down with the other hand. I closed my eyes as my aunt placed the veil on my head. It was the final adornment that had to be put on before my walk down the aisle. She pulled it over my face and I took a step toward the door.

I was nervous, anxious, and giddy. I was completely unaware of the journey that lay before me. But I was ready.

My husband and I will celebrate fifteen years of marriage this year. Over those years, we have given and taken, hurt and healed, laughed and loved and learned to do better. These few paragraphs are not nearly enough space to hold all that I owe my husband. But my largest debt to him is this: he has made me ready to meet my Savior.

Because of Tom, I know the tangible feeling of heavenly forgiveness. I've witnessed countless acts born from a servant's heart. And I've been held steady through the storms of life more times than I can count. My faith is stronger because Tom has loved me well.

I will run wildly into the arms of my Savior when He calls me home, because I've experienced earthly realities of His love for fifteen years. I know the moment when I see Jesus face to face will be glorious, because I've seen glimpses of Him in the man I am privileged to call mine.

Whether you are married or not, the choices that we make today are not just meant to prepare our own hearts for Christ. We exist to walk our fellow brothers and sisters right up to the moment when Jesus calls them home. We won't have any higher calling than that one.

Let us all be ready to step into it.

"NEITHER," HE REPLIED. "I HAVE NOW COME AS COMMANDER OF THE LORD'S ARMY." THEN JOSHUA BOWED WITH HIS FACE TO THE GROUND IN

WORSHIP AND ASKED HIM, "WHAT DOES MY LORD WANT TO SAY TO HIS SERVANT?"

JOSHUA 5:14

Turn in your Bibles to **Joshua 5 and read verses 13-14.**

Several years ago, I visited Paris with one of my dearest friends. It's a city surrounded by a river, so it's also a city surrounded by bridges. Every one of them has its own distinct personality, design, and custom views. Think back on your travels in life. Is there a bridge that you can recall that left a lasting impact in your mind? _____

To the left and the right of the bridge below, write what was on either side of your bridge that you thought of:

Consider the following quote from Kenneth Matthews about the book of Joshua:

THE BOOK OF JOSHUA SERVES AS A BRIDGE BETWEEN THE ACCOUNTS OF ISRAEL'S LIFE OUTSIDE THE LAND OF CANAAN AND THOSE OF ITS LIFE INSIDE THE LAND.

Okay, now summarize Matthews' quote below by filling in either side of the bridge below, similar to what you just did with the one above.

If you grew up in the Christian church, you might have heard your youth group pastor describe our relationship with Jesus in this way: *Jesus is the bridge from us to God.* If you aren't familiar with that comparison, these verses help to illustrate that concept. Choose three of the verses below and then use details from the verses you chose to fill in either side of the bridge below them.

1 TIMOTHY 2:5

1 PETER 4:1-2

JOHN 14:6

1 JOHN 2:1

ROMANS 8:34

HEBREWS 7:24-25

Okay, hold those thoughts for a moment. Now, turn back to **Joshua 5 and reread verses 13-14**.

Who appeared to Joshua here? _____

How did Joshua respond? _____

_____

If you participated in the teaching session for this week, you'll remember that the appearance of the commander of the Lord's army here in **Joshua 5** is a theophany.

THEOPHANY:
A MANIFESTATION OF GOD THAT IS TANGIBLE TO THE HUMAN SENSES, OFTEN A VISIBLE APPEARANCE OF GOD IN THE OLD TESTAMENT.

We have seen the foreshadowing of the first coming of Christ, on multiple occasions throughout our study of **Joshua 1-5**. If you can recall a few, list them here:

While scholars disagree as to whether or not this is the appearance of the *preincarnate Christ* in **Joshua 5**, they all agree that what Joshua is seeing here is the physical appearance of God right before his eyes.

PREINCARNATE:
OF, RELATING TO, OR HAVING EXISTENCE BEFORE INCARNATION —USED ESPECIALLY OF THE SECOND PERSON OF THE TRINITY, JESUS CHRIST.

Read **Joshua 5:14** below and underline what God says to Joshua:

I have now come....

These are words that stop me in my tracks every time I read this passage. They are words that Jesus will say on multiple occasions when He comes to earth for the first time. Choose three of the verses below to read and note to the right of each one what Jesus says about why He has come.

MARK 1:38

LUKE 5:32

JOHN 5:43

JOHN 10:10

JOHN 12:46

JOHN 18:37

These are words spoken by Jesus about his first coming to this earth. But the Bible promises that He is coming again.

Let us rejoice and be glad and give him glory! For the wedding of the Lamb has come, and his bride has made herself ready.

REVELATION 19:7 NIV

Take a moment to describe the scene that **Revelation 19:7** paints for us. What do you envision when you consider this verse?

Do you see yourself in this picture?

Sister, as a member of the body of Christ, you are the bride. Jesus will come for you and when He does, you will behold a glorious wedding. You will be exquisite and Jesus will be glorified.

I also saw the Holy City, new Jerusalem, coming down out of heaven from God, prepared like a bride adorned for her husband.

REVELATION 21:2

Jesus is coming again. Until that time, however, we are walking on a bridge of time between His first coming and His second. Take a moment to consider all that has happened in the first five chapters of Joshua. Maybe you'd even like to chart a timeline of the stories below.

Of the stories that we have studied, which ones have impacted you the most?

Would you be bold enough to consider that as we march along this current bridge of time, waiting for Jesus and ready for His return, that the story of your life will make a lasting impact on the kingdom of God?

Someone reading this study is a Joshua. God will place you in front of many to lead them home.

Someone reading this study is a Rahab. God will use your story to strike fear into the heart of the enemy.

Someone reading this study is an Israelite daughter. God will turn the memorial you leave to Him into a lasting legacy for your family.

LET'S WALK STEADY ALONG THE BRIDGE TO HELP OTHERS BE READY FOR CHRIST'S RETURN.

We'll close this day by asking God to (1) keep you steady as you walk along the bridge of life here on earth, and (2) to use you to help others be ready for His return.

JESUS' FIRST COMING   JESUS' RETURN

THEN HE SAID TO THEM, "GO AND EAT WHAT IS RICH, DRINK WHAT IS SWEET, AND SEND PORTIONS TO THOSE WHO HAVE NOTHING PREPARED, SINCE TODAY IS HOLY TO OUR LORD. DO NOT GRIEVE, BECAUSE THE JOY OF THE LORD IS YOUR STRONGHOLD."

NEHEMIAH 8:10

HOLY GROUND

I awoke that morning with little awareness that change was coming. I began my day with a series of gentle stretches like I always do. Cranky hips and ankles require some attention if one expects them to carry the weight of the day. A roll of the ankle here, and bend of the waist there. Slow and even breaths in between each movement offered a pep talk to joints that were hesitant to comply.

Songs from my praise and worship playlist adorned the air. I let the peaceful rhythm of the music set the pace for my stretches. Before too long, I found myself on my knees, face down on the floor with my palms turned upwards towards heaven. I stayed there, still and worshipping my heavenly Father, knowing that God was calling for surrender.

Surrender.

For many, it's not an easy word to muster. But when ready hearts are moved to surrender to the will of God, the ground beneath them changes from humdrum to Holy.

God moved swiftly in the days that followed. They would be marked by deep and cleansing change, but my life going forward would be permanently branded with purpose.

Surrender doesn't happen without a heaping dose of courage. But when we embrace the courage to step onto Holy ground, we find our true calling.

THE COMMANDER OF THE LORD'S ARMY SAID TO JOSHUA, "REMOVE THE SANDALS FROM YOUR FEET, FOR THE PLACE WHERE YOU ARE STANDING IS HOLY." AND JOSHUA DID SO.

JOSHUA 5:15

Turn in your Bibles to **Joshua 5 and read verse 15.**

What is Joshua asked to do in verse 15? _____

_____

Why is he asked to do this? _____
_____

Turn to read **Exodus 3:1-12.** List any similarities between **Joshua 5:13-15** and **Exodus 3:1-12** here:

Considering what you just wrote, what clues can you point to that confirm that the identity of the commander is in fact, God.

Now, let's take a closer look at those sandals.

Read **Deuteronomy 25:8-9** and **Ruth 4:7-8**. Based on what these verses say about sandals, what can you infer about what sandals might represent?

Why do you think the commander asked Joshua to remove his sandals?

If we have learned anything from Joshua, it is that godly leadership is marked by humility and submission to the will of God.

When my son was five, we had a writing spider build her web just outside our (thankfully) screened-in porch. She was close enough that we could watch her every day through the screen. Although she looked rather menacing, she was actually quite harmless. My son claimed her as our pet and named her Missy. We watched her entire life cycle before our eyes that summer, from her first web through the laying of her eggs to the days when she quietly disappeared to die. Through it all we read *Charlotte's Web* together to commemorate the experience.

In his book *Xealots: Defying the Gravity of Normality*, Dave Gibbons writes of Charlotte:

> AS THE STORY DRAWS TO A CLOSE, CHARLOTTE THE SPIDER IS IN THE BARN DYING, AND SHE CAN HEAR THE ROAR OF APPLAUSE FOR WILBUR THE PIG [AS HE WINS A PRIZE AND HIS LIFE IS SAVED]. CHARLOTTE FINDS GREAT JOY IN KNOWING THAT HER LIFE HAS MEANT THE SUCCESS OF ANOTHER, HER CLOSE FRIEND, WILBUR. THOUGH NO ONE WILL REMEMBER HER, THE THINGS SHE HAS DONE, AND THE SACRIFICES SHE HAS MADE, SHE IS SATISFIED, HAVING LOVED HER FRIEND IN LIFE AND DEATH.

Gibbons goes on to say of godly leadership, "*it's about fading. The great ones willingly move into irrelevance.*"

Joshua took to heart what we know is true of the Christian life:

HE MUST INCREASE, BUT I MUST DECREASE.

JOHN 3:30

Glance ahead at the sixth chapter of Joshua and jot down what is about to happen:

We are leaving our story just as Joshua marches into Jericho. The battle isn't over. The Israelites are on the cusp of another fight and it would appear to be an impassable one. But throughout this study, we've long since abandoned the perception that the unknown is insurmountable. The truth of these last few verses of **Joshua 5** surely reverberated in Joshua's heart, so we will let it resound in ours as well:

WHEN THE IMPOSSIBLE STANDS BEFORE US, THE COMMANDER OF THE LORD'S ARMY STANDS WITH US.

Remind yourself of Joshua's posture found in **Joshua 5:14**: _____

_____

His posture prepared him for the marching orders he was about to receive in **Joshua 6**. Let's assume the same one today. Glance up above at **John 3:30** and below at the two columns. Take some time to consider areas in your life that are in need a little humility. Areas in which you can bow before your God and trade your life for His glory.

As they come to mind, list them below in the appropriate column. I've given of few examples of my own to get you started.

LESS	MORE
Fear	Trust in God
Timidity	Boldness in sharing the love of Christ

HE MUST INCREASE, BUT I MUST DECREASE.

JOHN 3:30

Sisters, only one more day left of this study and I am so proud of you! Go into today knowing that the commander of the Lord's army stands with you.

Day Five
ANOTHER WORD FOR READY

Get ready.

When I think about the way God graciously prepared my heart with those two simple words, I have to close my eyes and catch my breath. Of course, my husband and I had no idea what kind of battle we were walking into when I made my first of many emergency room visits. But because God had planted His commands and His promises in our hearts, we were ready.

When I had two aneurysms a few weeks later, we were ready. When I started chemotherapy intended to fix what we thought was an auto-immune disorder, we were ready. When my carotid artery ruptured, we were ready. When I was transferred very quickly to a larger hospital because my local hospital was not equipped to deal with me, we were ready. When my surgeon told us that the procedure required to fix my artery was extremely risky for someone with my condition, and that it might take more than one surgery to fully repair it, we were ready. When I whispered words of mother wisdom to my son, not knowing if I would see him again, I was ready. When my husband held my hand before they took me back to the operating room to start the second surgery, I told him I was ready. When the genetics team at UNC prepped my arm for the blood draw to test my DNA, I was ready. When the phone rang with the results that I did indeed have an incurable genetic disorder, we were ready.

When we walked through moments of fear and doubt, which certainly lurked around every corner, we were ready for God's grace and mercy that was flooded upon us.

And when we watched God answer the hundreds of prayers lifted up on my behalf, we were ready and we rejoiced!!! Because we knew...*we knew*...that God was behind it all.

We were ready for all of these things not because we had a specific skill set, strength, or awareness that is different from anything that you possess now, but because God Himself was swinging the sword for us at every step along the battlefield. Our job was simply to be *faithful*.

AND JOSHUA DID SO.

JOSHUA 5:15B

Sisters, we have reached the last day of our study together! I wish I could hug your neck right now! I am so proud of you!!! More importantly, so is your heavenly Father. Can you hear these words ringing over you today?

"His master replied, 'Well done, good and faithful servant! You have been faithful with a few things; I will put you in charge of many things. Come and share your master's happiness!'

MATTHEW 25:23 NIV

You have been faithful! God is delighting over you today.

I've got a few final words for you in the closing section of this study, but for our last official day of homework together, I want to show you one of my favorite traits about Joshua's character. To find it, we'll have to skim through all of the five chapters of this book of Joshua that we have been studying.

Here's what I'd like you to do:

In the table below, you will find a list of passages to read. Each passage contains one of two things: a command from God and a response from Joshua. I'd like you to read each passage and note in the table below what God commanded Joshua to do and what Joshua's response was. Pay particular attention to how Joshua responded and the timing of his response. If some of God's commands are lengthy, it's okay to quickly summarize them. Our goal for today is to focus on Joshua's response.

Ready? 😊

READ	GOD'S COMMAND	READ	JOSHUA'S RESPONSE
Joshua 1:1-9		Joshua 1:10-11	
Joshua 3:7-8		Joshua 3:9-13	
Joshua 4:1-3		Joshua 4:4-7	
Joshua 4:15-16		Joshua 4:17	
Joshua 5:2		Joshua 5:3	
Joshua 5:15		Joshua 5:15	

What patterns did you notice in Joshua's responses?

I think we can find a perfect summary of Joshua's behavior by glancing ahead at **Joshua 11:15**. Rewrite it word for word here:_____

_____

_____

_____

_____

Joshua 11:15 refers to Joshua's fulfillment of what the Lord had spoken to Moses, but it perfectly describes Joshua's responses also to the Lord. He left *nothing undone*. He was faithful to His God.

Girls what a testimony that would be! To arrive at the throne of Jesus and have Him say that we left *nothing undone* that He commanded of us. I've seen the darkest pits of this broken world. I know how lofty that goal will be. But nevertheless, that is my goal. And because we have these truths from Joshua's story deep in our hearts, we know that it is attainable. Not because we possess anything special ourselves, but because we can rely on the one true God to get us through every single unknown in our future.

FAITHFUL HEARTS ARE READY HEARTS.

Merriam-Webster's Dictionary defines the word *faithful* in this way:

FAITHFUL:
LOYAL, CONSTANT, STAUNCH, STEADFAST, RESOLUTE, FIRM IN ADHERENCE TO WHATEVER ONE OWES ALLEGIANCE.

Based on our study of **Joshua 1-5**, how would you define *faithful*?

And how would you define *ready*?

Sisters, take these definitions into your unknown today. You have all that you need to be ready for whatever comes your way, because your heavenly Father stands with you. Ready.

SHE IS CLOTHED WITH STRENGTH AND DIGNITY, AND SHE LAUGHS WITHOUT FEAR OF THE FUTURE.

PROVERBS 31:25 NLT

Closing Thoughts
ON BEING READY

On the day that I had planned to write these closing thoughts, I ended up in the emergency room instead. The reason was related to my medical condition and it turned out to be just a baby bump in the road, for which we were very grateful. But as I took in the sights and sounds around me that evening: the steady beeps of all the medical equipment around the gurney, the quick shuffle of feet as doctors and nurses hurried to help their patients, the sharp smell of sterile tools and antiseptic everything, and the click of the clock as we waited for unknown test results to return, all the truths of this study came crashing back in my mind.

Was I ready? Did I have the courage to face the unknown? Do you?

Can you eye the raging waters in front of you and step toe to water? Can you watch the arrows fly over your head and smile? Can you move forward into the unknowns of this world, ready, determined, unafraid, and untethered to this life, focused on God's purpose for you?

As you close the pages of this study, I hope you can answer yes to every one of those questions. The sheer reality of this life on earth is that the unknown beckons every day. You will undoubtedly face moments of uncertainty. When you do, you can return to the pages of Joshua to remind you of the same truths he learned from God that we learned together here.

Because the glorious reality of a life lived with God is that the unknown holds His presence. Within moments of uncertainty, you will also find moments of divine promise. God is looking for ready warriors, women who are willing to march boldly into the unknown.

Be strong. Be courageous.

You are ready.

Tools for Studying the Bible

I was a sophomore in college when I first learned that there were actual methods and tools for studying the Bible. Before then, Bible "study" meant reading a few verses and saying a quick prayer. Nothing wrong with that, mind you. But over the years I've gathered resources that help me deepen my understanding of God's Word. These are some of my favorites:

QUESTIONS TO ASK AFTER READING A PASSAGE FROM THE BIBLE

What does it say? What does it mean? What does it mean to me?
What does this passage tell me about the character of God the Father?
What does this passage tell me about Jesus?
What does this passage tell me about the Holy Spirit?
Who is the original audience for this passage?
What do I know about the cultural and historical background for this passage?
Are there literary patterns evident in this passage of scripture?
Does this passage point to other scriptures? Is this passage cross-referenced anywhere else?

ONLINE TOOLS

www.biblegateway.com – useful for reading large passages of scripture in different translations

www.biblehub.com – useful for comparing parallel translations of the same verse at once, and for researching the original meaning of the Greek or Hebrew of a particular word.

www.bible.com – app for mobile devices, useful for reading the Bible on the go. Try the audio versions to listen to scripture as you go about your day, or try one of the many reading plans they offer.

www.blueletterbible.org – useful for in-depth study of the Bible, with access to cross-references, commentaries, and dictionaries.

www.thebibleproject.com - an organization committed to making the Biblical story accessible to everyone. They produce creatively animated videos that explore the Bible as a unified story, always pointing to Jesus.

BOOKS

Women of the Word: How to Study the Bible with Both Our Hearts and Minds, by Jen Wilkin, Crossway

Essential Atlas of the Bible, by Carl Rassmussen, Zondervan

Holman Illustrated Bible Dictionary, by Chad Brand and Eric Mitchell, Holman Reference

Holman Illustrated Bible Commentary, by E. Ray Clenenden and Jeremy Royal Howard, Holman Reference

The New Strong's Expanded Exhaustive Concordance of the Bible, by James Strong, Thomas Nelson

VERSES TO PRAY OVER AS YOU STUDY THE BIBLE

2 Timothy 3:16-17 – All Scripture is inspired by God and is profitable for teaching, for rebuking, for correcting, for training in righteousness, so that the man of God may be complete, equipped for every good work.

Psalm 119:105 - Your word is a lamp for my feet and a light on my path.

Proverbs 2:1-5 - My son, if you accept my words and store up my commands within you, listening closely to wisdom and directing your heart to understanding; furthermore, if you call out to insight and lift your voice to understanding, if you seek it like silver and search for it like hidden treasure, then you will understand the fear of the LORD and discover the knowledge of God.

Hebrews 4:12 - For the word of God is living and effective and sharper than any double-edged sword, penetrating as far as the separation of soul and spirit, joints and marrow. It is able to judge the ideas and thoughts of the heart.

James 1:5 - Now if any of you lacks wisdom, he should ask God, who gives to all generously and without criticizing, and it will be given to him.

Acknowledgements & Gratitude

MY DEEPEST AND HEARTFELT THANKS TO...

My husband, Tom, for believing in me, for personally walking through every moment of this journey right by my side, and for loving me the way Jesus loves the church.

My son, Thomas, for being my fiercest cheerleader and for still giving the best of hugs even when I couldn't play as many games of Go Fish as I wanted to because I had to go work on my study.

My Turtle Sisters, for being the first to usher this study into the world and for faithfully serving as my editing crew. I will always cherish our time together in God's Word.

My Wake Cross Roads Baptist Church Ready gals, for spending your summer months walking through the first five chapters of Joshua with me and for forgiving me when I forget to brush my teeth. Our church is so blessed to have you ready warriors within its doors.

My dear friend, Lauren Gaskill of The Cocoa Creative, for formidably leading the book launch charge and for being the extrovert I've always dreamed of being. I owe you mounds and mounds of dark chocolate.

My book launch team, for helping me introduce this study into the world. Thank you for volunteering your time and resources and for handling this dream with joy and excitement.

And last, but certainly not least, to my precious friends and family who loved, fed, and prayed us through the valley from which this study was born. We are richly blessed in the fact that there are far too many of you to name, but you know who you are. If God credits me with any spiritual readiness at all, it will have only been because of you.

Leader Guide
TIPS AND RESOURCES FOR LEADING A GROUP

Thank you for investing your time and resources in leading others through the study of God's Word. I know from personal experience that the job is a rewarding one, but I also know that it requires an extra layer of thought, prayer, and preparation.

What follows here are tips, resources, and suggestions to help your group get the most out of your time together. The suggested outline below for your group time is just that, a suggestion. You will know best how to customize your time based on the needs of the women who are participating in the study.

Know that I am praying for wisdom, discernment, and blessing over you as you encourage women in their faith. Thank you for serving them.

BEFORE THE STUDY BEGINS
* Pray, pray, pray. Pray for the women attending your study, whether you know their names yet or not. Pray for their families. Pray for yours. Psalm 91 is a beautiful Psalm to pray over your group members and over your family as you move through Joshua, particularly as it has a significant connection to this study.
* Consider how many weeks you will be meeting. Consider holding a social gathering before and after the study to allow time for fellowship and community building.
* Consider whether or not food will be involved and/or served. If so, how much and who will provide it? Light refreshments? Potluck dinner? Four-course meal? (we can dream, right girls?) Plan accordingly.
* This seems obvious, but invite women to come! Think of your neighbor, your co-worker, your friend you haven't seen in a while. Ask God to place specific people on your heart and to go before you when you invite them to the group.
* If you are hosting the study in your home, go ahead and block out a few minutes to prepare on the days you are scheduled to meet. It has been my experience that women don't really care if there are cheerios on your carpet; what matters most is that your heart is ready to welcome them. Preserving time to get your materials ready and pray for your time together is helpful. Schedule that in your calendar as you can.

THE FIRST NIGHT THAT YOU GATHER

- ❖ Consider having nametags if your group is large or includes new faces.
- ❖ Collect emails (or other contact info) from your group. This will be helpful when you want to send some encouraging thoughts or need to change timing or meeting details. Items noted below as an EXTRA RESOURCE are good ideas to consider including in a weekly email.
- ❖ Spend some time in fellowship and allow time for introductions or catching up.
- ❖ Offer refreshments. They don't have to be fancy.
- ❖ Hand out workbooks and scripture cards. Printable scripture cards are available in the digital version of the Leader Guide, which can be found at www.therescuedletters.com/ready-leader.
- ❖ Ask the group what they are looking forward to most about the study, what drew them to study Joshua, etc. This will help you be sensitive to their needs as you guide them through God's Word.
- ❖ Briefly walk through ABOUT THE STUDY with them and make sure they understand there are different levels of participation for the study.
- ❖ If your group is active on social media, encourage them to use the hashtag #READYSTUDY to connect with other women doing the study.
- ❖ Ask for prayer requests and spend some time in group prayer.
- ❖ Pray Psalm 91 (from the INTRODUCTION) over them.
- ❖ Watch the teaching video for SESSION 1: A NEW WAY.
- ❖ EXTRA RESOURCE: Watch the Joshua summary video from The Bible Project: https://youtu.be/JqOqJlFF_eU

SECOND MEETING

- ❖ Go over any announcements that need to be made.
- ❖ Move into a time of discussion over the homework assignments from WEEK ONE. Suggested questions that discuss WEEK ONE homework are:
  - ○ ICEBREAKER: Tell us your name and also how long it takes you to get ready in the morning.
  - ○ DAY 1: Does knowing that God is a promise-keeper change the way you pray?
  - ○ DAY 2: Describe what you learned about Joshua from the experience in the chart you chose to study.
  - ○ DAY 3: Is God calling you to take the lead on something? If so, tell us about it. What is it your turn to do?
  - ○ DAY 4 We looked at the words *get ready* used in Joshua 1:2 from different translations. Describe in your own words what you think God was asking Joshua to do here.
- ❖ Ask for prayer requests and spend some time in group prayer.
- ❖ Watch the teaching video for SESSION 2: THE RIVER BANK YOU CAN'T SEE
- ❖ EXTRA RESOURCE: Play the worship song *Ready for You*, by Worship Central: https://youtu.be/842BA9R8_bY

THIRD MEETING

- ❖ Go over any announcements that need to be made.
- ❖ Move into a time of discussion over the homework assignments from WEEK TWO. Suggested questions that discuss WEEK TWO homework are:
  - o ICEBREAKER: When do you start getting ready for Christmas?
  - o DAY 1: Of the promises we looked at from Joshua 1, which one resonated the most with you and why? Bonus: share your rewritten promise in your own words.
  - o DAY 2: Do you think there is a difference between strength and courage? If so, why?
  - o DAY 2: Which verse did you choose to meditate on this week? Did that help you in any way throughout your week?
  - o DAY 3: What are the six P's of God's presence? Which one resonates the most with you today?
  - o DAY 4: What items would you put in your ready toolbox?
- ❖ Ask for prayer requests and spend some time in group prayer.
- ❖ Watch the teaching video for SESSION 3: A SCARLET CORD FOR ALL
- ❖ EXTRA RESOURCE: Watch the final battle scene from *The Chronicles of Narnia: Prince Caspian* (mentioned in the Session 3 teaching video): https://youtu.be/rkSUhTfxIt4

FOURTH MEETING

- ❖ Go over any announcements that need to be made.
- ❖ Move into a time of discussion over the homework assignments from WEEK THREE. Suggested questions that discuss WEEK THREE homework are:
  - o ICEBREAKER: How long does it take you to get dinner ready on a weeknight?
  - o DAY 1: How do you think Joshua's experience as a spy for Moses affected the decisions he makes as a leader in Joshua 2:1?
  - o DAY 2: What words come to mind when you think about Christ's return? Does it make you anxious or hopeful? Do you think you will be ready?
  - o DAY 3: How does God use Rahab to bring hope into the world?
  - o DAY 3: Choose one of the verses you rewrote and share why it resonated the most with you.
  - o DAY 4: We spent some time exploring the imagery and history of the Passover connecting the Old and New Testaments, and in particular, Jesus' role as our Passover and securer of our salvation. Did the study of the Passover change, influence, or enhance your view of the Bible and God's plan for humanity?
- ❖ Ask for prayer requests and spend some time in group prayer.
- ❖ Watch the teaching video for SESSION 4: PUT ME ON THE FRONT LINE
- ❖ EXTRA RESOURCE: Play the worship song *Dominion*, by Citipointe Live: https://youtu.be/AtaBXeQW3FA

FIFTH MEETING

- ❖ Go over any announcements that need to be made.
- ❖ Move into a time of discussion over the homework assignments from WEEK FOUR. Suggested questions that discuss WEEK FOUR homework are:
  - ○ ICEBREAKER: How many bags do you pack when you get ready to go on vacation for a week?
  - ○ DAY 1: What do you think the Israelites might have been thinking as they were about to cross the Jordan River?
  - ○ DAY 2: Which one of the six P's of God's Presence do you think would have resonated the most with the Israelites just before the crossing and why?
  - ○ DAY 3: We looked at two of the reasons why the ark travelled ahead of the Israelites. Which one of these resonated the most with you and/or what else do you think might be accomplished by having the ark travel so far ahead?
  - ○ DAY 3: Choose one verse that you read about the character of God. What did it tell you about Him?
  - ○ DAY 5: Where is God calling you into the unknown?
- ❖ Ask for prayer requests and spend some time in group prayer.
- ❖ Watch the teaching video for SESSION 5: TIME TO RISE
- ❖ EXTRA RESOURCE: Share the tools available from *The Bible Project* about the Holy Spirit: https://thebibleproject.com/explore/holy-spirit/

SIXTH MEETING

- ❖ Go over any announcements that need to be made.
- ❖ Move into a time of discussion over the homework assignments from WEEK FIVE. Suggested questions that discuss WEEK FIVE homework are:
  - ○ ICEBREAKER: What do you listen to when you get ready in the morning?
  - ○ DAY 1: We looked at what Promised Land living looks like for us, specifically our inheritance as it is defined in *riches* and *rest*. We ended our time on this day with a prayer asking God to reveal areas of riches and avenues of rest. Based on what He revealed, do you feel like you are walking in Promised Land living today? Why or why not?
  - ○ DAY 2: Review Alexander Whyte's quote at the top of the page. Do you agree with that statement? Why or why not?
  - ○ DAY 3: Share with us an item or two that you added to your Ebenezer Memorial?
  - ○ DAY 4: How would you describe the work of the Holy Spirit in your life thus far?
  - ○ DAY 5: What two words did you choose to sum up the entire fourth chapter of Joshua?
- ❖ Ask for prayer requests and spend some time in group prayer.
- ❖ Watch the teaching video for SESSION 6: THE BRIDGE, THE BRIDE, & THE PRIZE

❖ EXTRA RESOURCE: Play the worship song *Even So Come*, by Kristian Stanfill: https://youtu.be/fBHcvJhc6Pk

FINAL MEETING
- ❖ Go over any announcements that need to be made.
- ❖ Move into a time of discussion over the homework assignments from WEEK SIX. Suggested questions that discuss WEEK SIX homework are:
  - o ICEBREAKER: What will you remember most from your study of Joshua?
  - o DAY 1: What thoughts came to mind as you considered that the language behind the Hebrew word for *covenant* implies *a cutting* and that the physical expression of God's covenant with His Old Testament people was circumcision? In what ways does God ask the same of us (a cutting away of something) today?
  - o DAY 2: What does the "produce of Canaan" look like for you? Share how you have observed it showing up in your own life over the past six weeks.
  - o DAY 3: What do you envision when you consider the scene that Revelation 19:7 paints for us?
  - o DAY 4: Share a few thoughts you wrote down in your chart as you considered areas in your life that could be traded for God's glory. What showed up in your "less" column and what showed up in your "more" column"?
  - o DAY 5: Review the chart where you studied Joshua's responses to God's commands. What patterns did you notice in Joshua's responses? Do you see the same patterns evolving in your own life?
- ❖ Ask for prayer requests and spend some time in group prayer.
- ❖ Watch the brief wrap-up video.
- ❖ EXTRA RESOURCES: Encourage your members to deepen their study of Joshua with the following resources:
  - o Continuing to read the entire book of Joshua.
  - o Search for #READYSTUDY on social media to read the thoughts and perspectives of others who have done the study.
  - o *A Lineage of Grace*, by Francine Rivers (fiction, a retelling of the stories of five women from the Bible. The second story, *Unashamed*, is about Rahab.)
  - o *Called to Be God's Leader,* by Henry Blackaby and Richard Blackaby (nonfiction, a discussion on the character of Joshua and what we can learn from Him as we move forward into leadership roles.)

Once the study is over, think of ways to stay connected as a group. Plan a social gathering, have a night reserved just for prayer, or get involved in a service opportunity together. And then, decide what Bible study you will do next!

Continue to walk through God's Word together and you'll be rewarded with a precious sisterhood and a fulfilling relationship with your personal Savior.

Blessings to you as you move forward in His will.

Toe to water until Christ calls me home,

Heather

To receive a digital version of this leader guide, please visit: www.therescuedletters.com/ready-leader.

Endnotes

WEEK 2

1. Mathews, K. A. Introduction. *Joshua*. Grand Rapids, MI: Baker, 2016. 4. Print.

WEEK 3

1. Got Questions Ministries. 'What Is the Passover Lamb? How Is Jesus Our Passover Lamb?" *GotQuestions.org*. Got Questions Ministries, 04 Jan. 2017. Web. 1 Mar. 2017. <https://www.gotquestions.org/Passover-Lamb.html>.

WEEK 4

1. Consecrate. (n.d.) In *Merriam-Webster's collegiate dictionary*. Retrieved from http://www.merriam-webster.com/dictionary/consecrate
2. Bentorah, Chaim. 'For Whom My Soul Loves: A Hebrew Teacher's Journey to Understanding God's Love." *Chaim Bentorah*. Chaim Bentorah, 23 Sept. 2014. Web. 15 Mar. 2017. <http://www.chaimbentorah.com/2014/09/hebrew-word-study-shooting-arrow/>.
3. *Living Proof Live*. By Beth Moore. North Carolina, Greensboro. 2002. Conference.

WEEK 5

1. Wiersbe, Warren W. *Be Strong: Putting God's Power to Work in Your Life*. Colorado Springs, CO: David C. Cook, 2010. 24. Print.
2. Ibid, 24.
3. Robinson, Robert. "Come, Thou Fount of Every Blessing." *The Baptist Hymnal*. Nashville, TN: Convention, 1991. 98. Print.
4. Mackie, Timothy, and Jonathan Collins. "The Holy Spirit - The Bible Project." *The Bible Project*. The Bible Project, 08 Apr. 2017. Web. 15 Apr. 2017. <https://thebibleproject.com/the-holy-spirit/>.

WEEK 6

1. "Joshua - Easton's Bible Dictionary." Blue Letter Bible. *Easton's Bible Dictionary*, n.d. Web. 15 Apr. 2017. <https://www.blueletterbible.org/search/Dictionary/Joshua>.
2. "Covenant - Easton's Bible Dictionary Online." Bible Study Tools. *Easton's Bible Dictionary*, n.d. Web. 15 Apr. 2017. <http://www.biblestudytools.com/dictionaries/eastons-bible-dictionary/covenant.html>.
3. "Leo Tolstoy." *BrainyQuote.com*. Xplore Inc, 2017. 15 April 2017. https://www.brainyquote.com/quotes/quotes/l/leotolstoy121890.html
4. Mathews, K. A. Introduction. *Joshua*. Grand Rapids, MI: Baker, 2016. 10. Print.
5. "Theophany - Baker's Evangelical Dictionary of Biblical Theology Online." Bible Study Tools. *Evangelical Dictionary of Theology*, n.d. Web. 15 Apr. 2017. <http://www.biblestudytools.com/dictionaries/bakers-evangelical-dictionary/theophany.html>.
6. Preincarnate. (n.d.) In *Merriam-Webster's collegiate dictionary*. Retrieved from http://www.merriam-webster.com/dictionary/preincarnate
7. Gibbons, Dave. *Xealots: Defying the Gravity of Normality*. Grand Rapids, MI: Zondervan, 2011. 145-46. Print.
8. Faithful. (n.d.) In *Merriam-Webster's collegiate dictionary*. Retrieved from http://www.merriam-webster.com/dictionary/faithful

Made in the USA
Coppell, TX
28 April 2024

31802744R00109